LOVE LETTERS
TO
DANGEROUS
CHRISTIANS

LOVE LETTERS
TO
DANGEROUS
CHRISTIANS

By Mario Murillo

ANTHONY DOUGLAS PUBLISHING
P.O. Box 30427
Stockton, California 95213

LOVE LETTERS TO
DANGEROUS CHRISTIANS

Copyright @ 1994 By Mario Murillo

Published by Anthony Douglas Publishing,
P.O. Box 30427
Stockton, CA 95213-0427

ISBN # 0-9639982-2-6
PRINTED IN THE UNITED STATES OF AMERICA

TABLE OF CONTENTS

Forward and Dedication

It is <u>dangerous when Christians actually apply their faith to the real world</u>. It is dangerous when believers define the time between Sundays as the real Christian life.

The lethargic become lethal when they surmount personal emotions of God make up the worldwide family of Mario Murillo Ministries. We share a vision like a love affair. They have built a ministry that applies God's cure where it matters - - in the mainstream of secular life.

Our family is very opinionated. They expect our outreaches to combine piercing preaching, overwhelming worship, and verified miracles. They are especially threatening to evil because they are convinced we can win this war. But their most potent quality is <u>their conviction that they are a vital key to God's work</u>. They cannot spectate; they must act. They are <u>high impact disciples</u>.

Each month I write them a letter; this is my great challenge and joy! I picture these awesome saints from all walks of life. They hurt and they laugh, they are raising children in adversity, sometimes alone, they pray for me and share of their livelihood to make our soul-winning mission possible.

Whenever I write them I try to provide a window to what their love gifts are doing. I try to feed their hunger for more of Jesus. I write about things that are going on and what we must do about them. I try to instruct them on the weapons of our warfare.

These times are dangerous! The answer is not to run and hide but to become a greater threat to the darkness than it is to us. This breed understands this. They want no froth or filler but truth that brings them joy, holiness, and authority in Jesus.

This book is a compilation of my favorite love letters to my worldwide family, and it is also dedicated to them. Try not to read more than one letter a day so you can savor and absorb the truths they bear.

Of course some these letters are controverial! You always open your heart to dear friends. Jesus once said to Peter, *"Simon, Simon! Indeed, Satan has asked for you, that he may sift you as wheat, But I have prayed for you, that your faith should not fail..."* (Luke 22:31-32)

These, my friends, are the times that sift men's souls! In these pages you will find the unvarnished truth about these evil days and I will mark out a path that avoids the landmines and leads to clear victory. Make no mistake, I will get in your face, I will tell you not to halt at mere survival but to move up into supernatural emotions, peace, power, and gifts so that even Satan admits you are dangerous!

I. ARE YOU A CATALYST OR A SPONGE?

Dear Friends,

Important question ... maybe the most important question of this decade.

Look at life. The present social setting in America is an indescribable bombardment of stress, anger, violence and perversion.

Our daily dosage of toxic spiritual substances is greater than what prior generations endured in a whole year. We are watching America sink into a vat of emotional extremes.

It used to be that our values as a nation eroded gradually. Now they are being dismantled in wholesale lots. Here is a chilling example of what happened in just one week:

> **The Supreme Court rules that prayer is a threat to young minds, just as McDonald's hamburgers begins a promotion to influence three to six-year-olds to go see a Batman movie where the penquin character bites off a man's nose and blood spurts everywhere.**

The Christian today must possess a supernatural edge to navigate modern America. The toll on our spiritual bearings will be great if we are not divinely redesigned to handle the noxious fumes of this perverse generation.

Without an inward dynamic, what happened to Lot in Sodom can happen to us today. The Bible says Lot's soul was vexed. That vexation was no mere disgust or anger toward the sin around him; it was a grinding assault on his sense of right and wrong. When the perverted men of the city wanted to rape the angels that were sent to rescue Lot and his family, Lot offered to let them abuse his own daughters. His priorities as a father were muddled because he had sponged up some of the poison from Sodom.

In Matthew 24:4 says, "... *Take heed that no one deceives you.*" The original word in the Greek is "planeo". Planeo is a deception where you are bent off course. Ancient travellers knew that if your horizon or "plane" was off by just a couple of degrees, you could be thrown off course by hundred of miles.

When Satan cannot stop you or get you to believe a lie, he will, instead, simply bend your direction slightly. Before you know you can be way off course.

Examples of this bending effect are rampant. More than ever, Christian singles are sleeping around. Too many ministers are indulging in stories that are just plain raunchy. The deception is, that compared to the current decadence, these actions look like minor sins when, in fact, they are disasters in the making.

Beyond this, many of God's people are depressed, despairing and they carry the same open sores of this pagan society.

So, I ask again: are you a sponge or a catalyst? Is this present darkness taking a toll on your emotions, maybe even your sanity? Are you soaking up today's poisons?

What is the difference between a catalyst and a sponge? A sponge absorbs, and a catalyst emits. A sponge takes on the color, odor and flavor of what is going on around it. A catalyst, the dictionary says, is *"any element that changes what surrounds it without itself undergoing a change."*

The most obvious difference between a Christian who is a sponge and one who is a catalyst is the sponge allows what's on the outside to seep in and destroy what's on the inside. A catalytic Christian draws on what is within to neutralize the poisons that come from outside. The most radical example I can think of is that of the Hebrew children coming out of the furnace without even the smell of smoke on them. The Book of John speaks of a fountain. This fountain within is the exclusive property of born-again Christians! Jesus said it will *"well up to everlasting life."* These overflows are our retaliation to the toxins of daily living. Catalytic faith says, *"though our outward man perish, our inward man is renewed day by day."*

Let's look at the miserable life of a sponge./The sponge succumbs to moods created by the whims of life. They are subject to whatever life may impose on them. Even before disaster strikes, they are already paralyzed by fearful pictures in their imagination. They are continually off-balance, never able to get a grip as they bounce from trauma to trauma.

Their agenda is set by forces outside them and they react accordingly. The sponge can't finish projects and can't keep promises they make to themselves. The sponge can't break a habit.

The sponge rehearses past hurts, nurses grudges and re-lives betrayal, soaking in every drop of pain. The sponge acquires all the latest phobias and syndromes.

Sponges can even set up their friends to fail them. They live out a scenario of self-fulfilling prophecy. They expect life to be a downward spiral.

Catalysts do not react to their life - they act on it. The catalytic Christian knows that inward victory is the real victory. They have an inner fountain and an internal dynamo. This dynamo is their covenant with God! Operating instructions from the Bible and a living relationship with Jesus have been combined and forged into the center of their being. From this center they generate action - action that changes, diffuses and nullifies the multiple attacks on them. In short, the catalyst doesn't let Satan make the rules, set the agenda or define the meaning of their situation! From their Christ center they act on life and subjugate their problems to a divine perspective.

Jethro, the father-in-law of Moses, advised the frazzled leader succinctly, *"Be to the people Godward."* The catalyst's Godward bent fuels his victories!

Catalysts can go anywhere, anytime, and do whatever needs to be done when it needs to be done. Criticism doesn't cripple them, it launches them. They eat the chicken of life and spit out the bones. Past hurts are forgotten; they are closed episodes. Every day is a clean slate and success is available from every direction.

4

To become a catalytic Christian, you must embrace a truth that is at first painful but soon becomes your best friend. Life cannot hurt me without my permission. I cannot feel insulted unless I choose to. I cannot be brokenhearted until I have decided something has broken my heart. Any event, pain, or feeling that comes at me, regardless of how strong it is, still must get my permission to enter and hurt me.

The catalytic Christian makes building material out of anything that attacks him.

Taking complete responsibility for your life and affirming your power to choose means you stop blaming parents, friends, enemies and all of life itself for hurting you.

Blaming is the narcotic of the sponge. Believing they have no choice is what permits everything to seep in. Self-pity is a cheap thrill that always destroys.

Do these things to start the life of a catalyst:

1. **Life cannot defeat me without my permission. Believe it!** Philippians 4:13 says, "I can do all things through Christ who strengthens me." The might of Jesus within is the catalyst. He causes me to take captive my every experience and transform it into fuel for victory.

2. **Wear all the armor of God, all the time**. The armor will quench fiery darts and stop the poisons from entering my spirit. My morals will be guarded because I am in tune with Christ and not bent by degraded modern standards.

5

3. **I will not react to circumstances, but act on them**. Creative action will well up out of my spirit to change what's going on around me. The dynamo and the fountain within me will make things happen!

4. **I will put Christ at the center and redefine my life from that center**. Instead of jumping from crisis to crisis, I will stop and embrace a Godward perspective. I will be moved by a deep strategy and not panic impulses. I will move forward, ever mindful of the heavenly vision and my personal destiny.

My every crisis will surrender, in one way or another, to the inevitable victory of Christ.

A catalyst declares, *"The end times are not happening to me ... I am happening to the end times!"*

II. THE WEAPON OF CHOICE

Dear Friends,

In every generation, hell belches out a new device meant to damn souls. Just now, America writhes under Satan's most advanced weapon.

Heaven is not passive. God reacts by engineering His own weapon uniquely created to nullify the wicked scheme.

When thrust at the enemy, this warhead is irresistible. To David it was mere pebbles, for Samson, a jawbone, and for Joshua, a shout. These are what I call *weapons of choice.* Chosen not for their outward appearance but for their devastating effect on evil.

Above all, Satan dreads the moment that God's people discover the weapon whose time has come. Weapons of choice were things in the Old Testament. In the New Testament, they are *people.*

The church is rarely able to accept the strange vessels Jehovah chooses. Look at Acts 9:13-14: "Lord," Ananias answered, "I have heard from many reports about this man, how much harm he has done to Your saints in Jerusalem. And here he has authority from the chief priests to bind all who call on Your name." Believers were fearful and dazed by how God chose the former murderer, Saul of Tarsus, to be the foremost weapon of evangelism.

John Wesley's methods shocked the Anglicans. Charles Finney, though he was our most effective evangelist ever, was

7

rejected by certain mainline denominations. History dilutes the radicalism of these men. We forget the most important lesson their lives taught us — that a weapon of choice does not come to get church popularity. It's only purpose is to pierce the darkness.

Mario Murillo Ministries has surrendered to the Holy Spirit to be redesigned, fitted and armed to attack the current wickedness. After pruning and empowering, we have emerged with key truths that I want to give you. These truths can transform you from a mere Christian to a weapon of choice.

1. **Seek to become a weapon above the pursuit of emotional well being**.

   Do not make emotional recovery a preoccupation. Here is a surprise attack on your past hurts and depression: *cast the spirit of suicide out of a suffering teenager.* I am not being sarcastic. I mean it! Your own depression cannot survive your act of giving life to others! Every time the anointing in us touches another life, a part of the blessing splashes back on us to meet our own needs. There is an important place for therapy so long as it moves the patient to recovery and not morbid self-analysis.

2. **Find out what kind of weapon you are**.

   You may not even know yourself! Gideon was a wimp in his own eyes but the angel declared his true weapon status. " The Lord is with you, you mighty man of valor!" (Judges 6:12). What God says you are will almost surely defy your view of yourself and the view others have of you.

8

Something will boil up from you as you pray. Write down the vision. It will come with clarity and power. Do not fear the strangeness or newness, and do not underestimate the Lord's power to make you lethal!

3. **Choose the right target**.

How can you explain the irony of Paul being told by Jesus in Acts 22:18 " ... *and I saw Him saying to me, Make haste and get out of Jerusalem quickly, for they will not receive your testimony concerning Me.*" Here was a totally religious city that yet was dangerous to vessels of God! Then in Acts 18:9-10: "Now the Lord spoke to Paul in the night by a vision, 'Do not be afraid, but speak, and do not keep silent; for I am with you, and no one will attack you to hurt you; for I have many people in this city.'"

Paul was commanded to target the most immoral city of that day - Corinth. This is like being told to leave Tulsa and go to San Francisco.

A weapon of choice abandons conventional thought in favor of divinely revealed targets! Why does this ministry go where it goes? Because, by choosing the right target, we can expect power and results. Are we here to be the darling of Christian circles, or are we here to save America?

4. **Attack**!

The single most important quality a soldier has is the will to attack. No amount of training or superior weaponry will matter if the soldier does not fire on the enemy. After all the preparation for "D-Day" in 1944, many lives were unnecessarily lost on Omaha Beach. This was because 80% of our army never fired their weapons. A decisive victory was bogged down by well-trained soldiers who simply did not attack!

Now that you know who you are and what you are to do, doing it becomes everything. Do not belittle your gift. Do not agonize over the exotic way God chooses to use you. Attack!

In every true Christian there lurks a warrior waiting to get out. You serve a mighty God who is waiting to counter today's evil through people — people like you!

III. WE CANNOT BE SAFE SO LONG AS WE ARE SECURE

Dear Friends,

Just now the people of earth are going to indescribable extremes in reaction to the convulsions of modern times.

Our Master warned us to guard our hearts for just an occasion as this: "But take heed to yourselves, lest your hearts be weighed down with carousing, drunkenness, and cares of this life, and that day come on you unexpectedly." (Luke 21:34)

But there is far more going on here than a mere warning of a heavy heart, and we must listen to it:

1. First, it is a warning about how the pagan frenzy for security and relief can spill over onto believers and weigh them down.

2. It is a warning of how a heavy heart can turn what should be our ultimate joy into a trap; that is, the second coming of Christ.

3. It is also a warning about awakening ... the same way that heavyhearted saints can be "trapped by the second coming" so we can be so loaded down by what is going on that we will be snared by our heart and literally oppose the awakening when it comes.

We must learn the life and death distinction of two words: (1) security and (2) safety.

Security: Seeking relief from uncertainty by acquiring money and power. Security is a quick fix, a painkiller. The irony of pursuing security is that you gain short-term relief, but you ultimately collide with the exact danger you most wanted to avoid.

Safety: Living in obedience to God which gives us actual freedom from danger. Christians obtain safety by placing their lives at divine risk. "... he who loses his life for My sake will find it." (Matthew 10:39)

"So long as we are secure," Matthew Henry warned, "we cannot be safe."

"Now if God so clothes the grass of the field, which today is, and tomorrow is thrown into the oven, will He not much more clothe you, O you of little faith? Therefore do not worry, saying, 'What shall we eat?' or 'What shall we drink?' or 'What shall we wear?' For after all these things the Gentiles seek. For your heavenly Father knows that you need all these things. But seek first the kingdom of God and His righteousness, and all these things shall be added to you." (Matthew 6:30-33)

In these verses Matthew affirms that God wants to give us the best of everything. He does not want us to seek these things simply as ends in themselves. At the root of material-ism is a fear of want, a security move born out of unbelief.

It is equally wrong to preach against having creature comforts, because abundance comes to those who seek the Kingdom.

Nowhere in the Bible is the contrast of security and safety more obvious than in Esther's life. She was the queen and her people faced genocide. She could save them but only by going to the king uninvited. If the king refused her, she would die. Her cousin, Mordecai said, "Do not think in your heart that you will escape in the king's palace any more than all the other Jews. For if you remain completely silent at this time, relief and deliverance will arise for the Jews from another place, but you and your father's house will perish..." (Esther 4:13-14)

The palace was Esther's temptation to security, but speaking out was her only means of safety.

There are many examples of safety versus security. Here are four of what I believe are our greatest temptations to security in this evil time:

1. **The security of withholding versus the safety of giving**. The only subject Jesus referred to more often than money was love. Financial security and financial safety are poles apart. Our money actions say volumes about us. Recessionary thinking in the unsaved has caused hoarding. In the child of God, holding back breeds disaster. Proverbs reveals it plainly: "There is one who scatters, (safety) yet increases more; and there is one who withholds more than is right (security), but it leads to poverty." (Proverbs 11:24)

   To cut out gifts to worthy causes to save money is a shortcut to the very disaster we want to prevent.

   In the coming outpouring, a stingy spirit can disqualify you. The generous heart wins on all counts. The giver has every advantage.

13

2. **The security of a career versus the safety of a mission.**
   There is nothing wrong with making money. In fact,
   success is promised in the Bible. But again our success
   cannot be the aggressive acquiring of wealth and power.

   To be sure, God wants us to be the best at what we do,
   but above all, it must be a mission.

   We must choose to serve and benefit humanity. A
   career only enhances you; a mission employs a strategy
   of meeting needs. Choose first to do good, then choose
   the vehicle for good, whether it will be through business,
   law, education, politics or ministry.

   Making lives better must take precedence over profits.
   Whether we are car dealers or pastors, our constituency
   must be served by our gifts. Ask yourself, "Is my
   occupation in any way blessing others?" If it isn't, you
   are secure but not safe.

3. **The security of silence versus the safety of loving
   confrontation.**
   While caustic bluntness is almost always wrong, silence
   in the face of injustice is equally disastrous. Silence can
   protect us but only for a little while. We dare not choose
   the "expedient" over the honest. The lies and double
   standards of today can crush right and wrong into an
   indistinguishable blob.

   The philosophy of homosexuality and abortion was
   inadvertently advanced by many Christian leaders who
   early on were squeamish about speaking out intelligently.
   They sought the security of compliance rather than the

safety of speaking out.

Micaiah was pressed in I Kings 22:13 to say what the other prophets were saying. But Micaiah said it for all of us when he replied, "As the Lord lives, whatever the Lord says to me, that I will speak." (I Kings 22:14)

Confrontation is a vital part of life. When it is done early, it can be done gently. Moreover, as you practice it, it becomes easier. After loving confrontation comes the reward of long-term peace. Honesty in relationships teaches us how to save a friend, not just a friendship.

"He who rebukes a man will find more favor afterward than he who flatters with the tongue." (Proverbs 28:23)

In our chosen field, we sacrifice immediate acceptance for the long-term respect that our positive frankness earns for us.

Liars carry a lot of baggage. They must have an exhaustive memory to keep their stories straight. The righteous can travel light in the end times.

4. **The security of popularity versus the safety of effectiveness.**

This is not about mere truthfulness but about the courage to act. The popular choose the actions that people like and will assure their being liked. The effective do what will work. Even the most seemingly sincere leader can choke on ideas that will work but are "politically sensitive."

We cannot set out to offend; we must live peaceably,

but in every crisis of life there are two constants:

    A. something is being done wrong;

    B. to correct it will offend someone.

Whether it is a personal renewal, a new form of evangelism, a business situation or political gridlock, change hurts.

The populist will rearrange the furniture but will not do anything meaningful. The effective Christian champions changes that will get the job done. Popularity can be a tool to bring effective changes so long as we are not seeking the security of being liked!There is a mighty storm of fresh fire coming to America. Do not give in to the extremes of lost America that is going on a binge of security, or you'll miss this glorious visitation.

Above all, we cannot be pulled by the current of modern fears. Isaiah said it best: *"Do not say, 'A conspiracy,' Concerning all that this people call a conspiracy. Nor be afraid of their threats, nor be troubled. The Lord of hosts, Him you shall hallow; Let Him be your fear, And let Him be your dread.* (Isaiah 8:12-14)

There it is. Do not fear what they fear, fear God and He Himself will become your safety!

IV. A TALE OF TWO SONS

Dear Friends,

I want you to see that the account of the prodigal son is far more than a story of repentance. Its other message is something that the church needs to see *now*.

Luke 15:11 says, "... A certain man had two sons. And the younger of them said to his father, 'Father, give me the portion of goods that falls to me.' So he divided to them his livelihood. And not many days after, the younger son gathered all together, journeyed to a far country, and there wasted his possessions with prodigal living."

This younger brother, driven by ambition, left home long before he was ready.

How did he know his father would give him his inheritance? This boy understood faith. The problem was, he didn't understand character.

Faith without character is when a person focuses on getting great things from God, but he has not developed inner integrity to handle the demands of success. This is the single greatest cause of wreckage among ministries.

We assume that if a man has a big ministry, he must be mature in Christ.

We can have faith yet lack true spirituality.
" ... and if I have faith that can move mountains, but have not love, I am nothing." (I Corinthians 13:2 NIV)

American Christians tend to worship results, and a string

17

of achievements can become a license to neglect our souls.

My heart is broken by the vast sums of money ministries have raised and squandered like a prodigals' inheritance.

Billions of dollars have trickled through our hands. Little that is meaningful has been done about America's darkness or about injustice and oppression in our communities.

Sadly, now more than ever, prodigal preachers have a following. For every ministry that has faith without character, there are thousands of sheep who overlook the shallowness.

Now, look at the older brother. His problem is the opposite extreme, and it is just as dangerous. He has character without faith.

Zacharias the priest "... walked in all the commandments and ordinances of the Lord blameless." (Luke 1:6). Yet this priest didn't believe the angel, Gabriel who appeared to him. His unbelief was so great that the angel struck him dumb (verse 20) until John the Baptist was born.

Character without faith is a decency that makes you apathetic about bold action.

We have millions of Christians here at home sitting back placidly, content to do nothing with their inheritance.

People who have character but no faith secretly grumble against those who dare to believe God. They tend to favor churches that stay small and programs that require no courage.

This rash of evangelists' scandals tragically fuel a lot of

righteous indignation against vision, but this reaction is nothing more than a fear to act on faith.

Why was the older brother still living at home? Maybe the younger brother got tired of this wimpy sibling and broke out.

The scriptures tell us that the father divided their inheritance. That means the older son also got his money. Yet later he whined that his father never gave him a party!

People who have character without faith tend to be technical experts on every abuse of faith and the gifts of God. Yet they themselves have never taken steps to appropriate miracles or do anything meaningful for the Kingdom of God!

The maddening part about these people is that they are always seemingly doing the right thing, but nothing effective or dangerous is ever done. And they are even willing to go to extremes to verify their purity. In I Corinthians 13:3 Paul said: "And though I bestow all my goods to feed the poor... but have not love, it profits me nothing."

You can give away all you own, but that only briefly helps the poor, and you become poor too. You can torch yourself and look holy, but what a meaningless death! People will go to these extremes rather than listen to God and do what will make a real difference.

For a long time I dismissed some "faith" preachers because they seemed arrogant, and they strutted like roosters when they preached. Though there are extremes in the faith movement, at the heart is a message for us: It is time we quit self-righteously staring at the promises of God. It is time to act on those promises.

Character without faith is a mass of moral effort that cannot help mankind.

Now we come to the summation of the whole matter: a deeper definition of love. Winkie Pratney says, "Love is willing the highest good for God and His universe." *Love insists on balance, because only balance will bring the highest good. Love* will provoke faith to add character, and love will demand that character add faith.

Paul said if I have faith but not love, " *I am nothing"*. But if I give everything away, without love, he adds that it "profits me nothing."

Without character you are nothing, and without faith you do nothing.

When we submit to the power of love, we will choose the golden way of being a person of both faith and character. When we start to produce vessels that can think *big* and *right*, we will change the world.

The love of God compels us to search ourselves and work on what we lack, not to gloat on what we abound in. May God speak to us today to combine these vital attributes into a mighty wholeness.

V. WE MUST DO THESE FIVE THINGS NOW!

Dear Friends,

I love the Spirit-filled Movement, but it faces a life and death situation.

Radical steps must be taken now to restore momentum, direction and balance in this movement. The devastating scandals must be faced squarely, and effective action is crucial.

History warns that we cannot be smug or casual about this crisis, or God will pass us by and wait to raise up another movement.

Our present dilemma mirrors an earlier threat to revival at the turn of the century. The Welsh revival leaped the ocean and struck America with holy force. City after city was revived, and the church added millions to her attendance rolls. By 1908, there were 600 evangelists crisscrossing the United States. Then a great embarrassment came to the Body of Christ.

Evangelists began to attack pastors and boast that they (the evangelists) needed no accountability. Money was abused, morals were abandoned, and finally, a crass commercialism overwhelmed mass evangelism.

The wind went out of the sails of the greatest awakening in American history. History will repeat itself without an intense redirection and change of heart!

Pentecostal revival or charismatic renewal — whatever you choose to call it — the issue is clear: the wind is going out of our sails.

In 1966, I observed firsthand the first stirrings of this movement in Southern California. Anaheim Christian Center was a small church, but Pastor Ralph Wilkerson soon saw thousands magnetically drawn to receive the baptism in the Holy Spirit.

This experience in God leaped denominational barriers. Books such as *The Cross and the Switchblade, They Speak with Other Tongues,* and *I Believe in Miracles* brought word of the Person of the Holy Spirit to millions.

What I saw happen in Los Angeles was being repeated everywhere across the United States. The movement was fueled by love, filled with joy, and shared by humble hearts. People touched people and celebrated their common ground in Christ.

The charismatics had a contagious gratitude to God that disarmed skeptics and won over much of the press.

What happened to this movement? Now we rarely speak of being baptized in the Holy Spirit. We have no more Holy Ghost rallies where the people are asked to come and receive this precious gift.

It is chilling to realize that we have spent over a billion dollars on television time and have seen only a fraction of the results we used to see when God broke out in communities and the secular media spread the word for us free of charge!

Charismatics and The Jesus Movement made the cover of magazines, were featured in prime time on networks, and all we had to do was obey God.

We must realize that the outpouring of God in the late sixties and mid-seventies made Christian television possible. But without a potent movement behind it, Christian television will end up a hollow tool.

I am convicted that we must restore the first love of this movement and recommit ourselves to the truths that give us life. To that end, I prescribe five things we must do now:

Point 1 - Stop Gossiping

Waiting to hear and discuss juicy details will poison your spirit. Not one of us has the wisdom or perfection to judge properly what punishment should be doled out to a fallen brother. We must pray wholeheartedly at this time for God's best and guard our own spirits from fatal attractions.

Sitting around analyzing the situation grieves God. There is no time for idle chatter at so critical a moment in our history.

Point 2 - Receive Fresh Fire

A great evangelical pastor recently said to a large group of charismatic pastors, "The greatest need you pastors have is to be filled with the Spirit." How ironic but how true. Our problem is so obvious that we have overlooked it completely!

Our success in using natural methods has distracted us from a vital dependency: experienceing repeated overflowings of the Spirit! We have a tradition that limits this power from on high to a once-in-a-lifetime experience.

After our initial baptism, we must have continual encoun-

23

ters of new overwhelmings of the Spirit. This is what I confronted in depth in my book, *Fresh Fire.*

When the man at the Gate Beautiful was healed, persecution threatened to destroy the church. Peter's reaction was unmistakable: call the people together to see a fresh enduement of power. And this was only two chapters after the Day of Pentecost!

Pastors need it. Evangelists need it. I need it. You need it.

But what did we do as a movement when we faced crisis? We formed committees; we raised money; we lashed back at the media; we hired lawyers.

What we have *not done* is the *only thing* we should do.

Go to God, repent of sin, and wait for power and a new tongue of fire!

Point 3 - Keep moving forward

No promise of God has been nullified. No Spirit-born vision has been cancelled. No soldier of God is disqualified from the promise of victory. Scandals have changed nothing vital. Therefore, keep moving forward. Your indecision and your confusion is Satan's only hope of lasting damage.

He wants to dismiss all men of God as phonies. He wants you to withdraw from being involved in effective ministry. He wants to gag your witness through embarrassment over being a Christian at this time.

If we retreat from witnessing, the public will only hear the media's side of the story. If we withdraw our involvement from sincere leaders, we punish the innocent along with the guilty. It's too easy to run away. The greatest danger at this time is the mass anti-vision mentality in the church.

We are right to be disenchanted by the "empire building spirit" but we must discern between human ambition and divine exploits.

These seven qualities are my test of a true vision of God:

- It is born out of a season of prayer, not just a good idea.
- It touches people directly. This includes feeding the poor, rescuing the oppressed and defending the weak.
- It complements the local church; it doesn't replace the local church.
- It expands to facilitate a growing impact on people; it does not get big for the   sake of bigness.
- It reveals Jesus and not side issues.
- It does not continually incur debt that overburdens the Body of Christ.
- It can be presented to wise counsel for confirmation.

No matter how impressed I am with a new project, I will not budge until it passes these seven tests.

Shall we punish the work of God in our day for the sins of a few? Never! Choose the ministries you support with careful prayer and faith. Do not retreat. The best is yet to come.

Point 4 - Seek protection

The Charismatic Movement has had two of its most visible leaders fall to immorality. It makes you wonder: if this has happened to the generals, what is the condition of the soldiers?

While we cannot judge the masses by the behavior of the few, we would be naive not to acknowledge widespread imbalance among charismatics.

If you think this is a time for just ministers to clean up their act, you are mistaken. You may not have a big ministry to worry about, but you still need to catch the warning of these events!

I don't believe that the loss of the public ministry is the greatest pain these men will face. There is the excruciating anguish of broken trust in their marriages plus the greater agony of knowing they have broken God's heart.

Spiritual shipwreck is a spectre that all of us face, from the greatest to the least. If Satan went after their spirit and their families, he will go after ours.

The principles of protection in scripture are there for a reason. Any individual who has not activated them is already in trouble! The clearest sign of danger is to think you don't need protection.

These are the principles of protection most overlooked by charismatics:

A. Loving Leadership That Can Tell You the Truth About Yourself

Isolation is the number-one killer of spiritual health. Proverbs 16:2 says, "All the ways of a man are pure in his own eyes." Human nature is blind to many of its own faults, so we need an objective outside opinion. Some people will only surround themselves with people who'll agree with them; this is suicide.

True leaders of God are truthful and encouraging. They will deal directly with falsehood but will leave you feeling stronger. Leadership like this, will not lord it over you. Submission is not slavery! Don't wait until you think you need them; seek them out now.

But be warned! Good leaders will not tolerate lip service. If you say you are under their care, then prove it by applying their good advice.

"Where no counsel is, the people fall; but in the multitude of counselors, there is safety." (Proverbs 11:14)

B. Study All the Bible: Learn the Important Doctrines of Faith

Too many Charismatics love instant guidance isolating single verses, and bending them to fit selfish ends.

However, without reading entire chapters and books of the Bible, wewill violate the context of a passage and reap confusion. Webster's dictionary defines "context" this way: "The parts just before and after a word or passage that determine its meaning."

When we rely on subjective experiences and buzz words and have little or no foundational knowledge of the Bible, we invite disaster. Instead, we should be searching scripture to build a solid base of truth that holds us steady even when we have no emotional experience.

"All scripture is given by inspiration of God, and is profitable for doctrine, for reproof, for correction, for instruction in righteousness." (II Timothy 3:16KJV)

C. Put On All the Armor

"Wherefore take up the whole armor of God, that ye may be able to withstand in the evil day, and having done all, to stand." (Ephesians 6:13)

Ephesians describes the *full* armor of God. Paul carefully names each piece of protection and then employs the word "all" in a significant way. Not just part of the armor can be worn, but all of it must cover us.

Charismatics have developed a casual attitude toward Satan by abusing scripture. Our enemy is defeated but still very talented. He knows human nature and relentlessly seeks ways to destroy us.

It's not so much what he can do to us, but what he can get us to do to ourselves.

An unguarded spirit and the presence of satanic influence is a lethal combination. I will leave it to others to theorize the full meaning of each piece of armor. But, in essence, Jesus Himself is the armor (Romans 13:14).

Paul's admonition can be boiled down to this: put on all the armor, all the time, and do all to stand.

Anyone who esteems himself above others will fall. If you make yourself the exception to the realities of war, you might as well wear a bull's eye.

Point 5 - Reconnect the Engine

We need a rude awakening. Let's start by rehearsing what a charismatic is and what gave us our early success.

"And it shall come to pass afterward, that I will pour out My Spirit on all flesh; your sons and your daughters shall prophesy, your old men shall dream dreams, your young men shall see visions. And also upon my menservants and on My maidservants I will pour out My Spirit in those days." (Joel 2:28,29 KJV)

A charismatic is a Christian who has experienced the outpouring of the Holy Spirit. They have received power but not just power! Charisma is the Greek word for gift. Charismatics are gifted ones.

God never gives gifts without intentions. All our scandals can be attributed to a basic violation: *we have simply not done what we were supposed to do with our gift.*

God poured out His Spirit on America in the late sixties to help prevent the social disaster of abortions, AIDS and drugs. God sent a cure, but we didn't fulfill our destiny.

Early on, we all shared - we all touched people. Then bad teaching blunted our momentum. We turned inward and became puffed up in pride over who we were.

The engine of this movement is the inner fire in each of us to be used of God.

As the movement became narcissistic, America plunged deeper into darkness. Instead of praying, "God, use me," we prayed, "God, bless me."

Now the signs of losing our first love are everywhere. We fight over trivial points of theology. Brothers attack brothers, and leaders jealously protect their turf. worked

The engine of this movement was a joyous fellowship. People were won by the love and joy they felt among us. Now, formality and division are the first things outsiders see.

I recall with fondness days when the presence of God was so sweet that it changed people. Now we must bribe them with promises of material blessing and social prestige.

The engine of this movement is a satisfied spirit. Jesus said to the woman, "You'll never thirst again." But we have ceased to believe it. We're living as though Jesus is not enough, as though the Spirit cannot empower. Yet I remember people so ablaze with Jesus and so overflowing with the Spirit that it made everything on earth seem so hollow.

If we do not recognize our desperate state and our need for a fresh vision of Christ and new anointing to what we're here to do, then the charismatic movement will soon end.

My great hope is that there are millions of charismatics who will put away foolishness and vanity to seek a new day of Pentecost that will yet rescue America.

VI. IS IT TOO LATE FOR AMERICA?

Dear Friends,

America is by far the wealthiest nation on earth, yet we are being strangled economically. We can airlift 500,000 soldiers, set up a mind-boggling fire power arsenal, and invade with blinding efficiency, but we can't stop crime at home.

We are the unquestioned champions of marketing and technology, and still we are falling behind the Japanese.

Our national crisis is as weirdly ironic as an Olympic swimmer drowning in a bathtub.

We are over-qualified, enriched, and full of opportunity to dwarf our crises and obliterate them.

The Soviet threat is largely gone and that should have freed up vast resources. The Desert Storm triumph should have spilled over into activism for our wars at home but neither has helped at all!

America has everything she needs to live, and yet she is dying ... dying for all the wrong reasons!

Something is cannibalizing our greatness. What is feeding on our will to live? Why are we walking with heads hung and voices that whine with a third world poverty mentality? Our credo was "can do," but now we are cattle. Our attitude has changed us from "the land of the free" to the club of "poor me."

Past Americans would not brood or dwell on whose fault something was; they would do whatever it took to solve the mess.

31

A power bloc of money interests has sold us down the river. Its "buy now, pay later; if it feels good, do it; quick-fix" values have enslaved us.

Are we a herd of consumer wimps who can't live above our glands? Have we given in to the compromiser, the bribe taker, the lazy intellectual, the half-baked expert, and the cold-blooded cynic?

America desperately needs courageous leaders whose words drop like a plumb line, voices free of corruption and regard for personal enrichment, who expose crooked and cracked foundations.

We need brave ideas, a return to sacrifice, voices of might, genius and dignity. We need proclaimers whose words will jettison us out of this economic Vietnam and our punch-drunk coma of pleasure. We need to dismantle the very machines of mediocrity and those committees that eat up wise solutions and censor common sense!

So where are these leaders? Who are these heroes? Where do we find new champions?

This will be the boldest declaration I've ever leveled at you through any letter. The people who read our newsletter each month are some of the most committed, creative, loving Christians in America! As I have traveled and talked with so many of you, I am humbled by the quality of people who are Mario Murillo Ministries supporters.

You are the heroes, the champions, the leaders America so desperately needs! That is the heart of this newsletter.

You must be great before it's too late for America!

We need greatness, not success! Success is the weak cousin of greatness. Success says, "I'm going to make a bunch of money and retire." Greatness says, "I'm out to make everyone's life better!"

"But, Mario, I'm old; I'm not that smart; I'm too young. I don't have time or opportunity." Can I be frank? **I have prayed that this letter would be to many of you what the burning bush was to Moses!** The bush was not consumed, but Moses' excuses were consumed.

So you must have your excuses burned up! Admit that greatness involves profound sacrifice; admit that pursuing it will upset every neat plan you have, and even further admit that greatness will endanger you. Yet I declare that far worse would be to ignore the call and lose your country by default.

For all the blood, sweat and tears of greatness, a far more painful outcome may await you: the cancer of regret, that voice that will haunt you from now on, asking over and over, "I wonder what would have happened if I had answered the call to true greatness?"

What excuse can I give my children for not fighting for their future?

The United States suffers at the hand of two kinds of people, those who rape her by greed and those who scurry away, unwilling to intervene.

So I ask: if not you, then whom? If not here, then where? If not now, then when?

33

If you've decided, here are seven things we can do to be great enough to save our nation.

1. **Know who you really are**!

   Gideon hid in a wine vat for fear of the Midianites. The angel called him to greatness right there and then. "... the Lord is with you, you mighty man of valor!" (Judges 6:12)

   Gideon had an identity bypass operation. It's what you need, as well. No one but God really knows you or your potential. Forget what parents, friends, I.Q. test scores and employers have said about you.

2. **Chart a bold and original course!**

   Who cares if it wasn't done this way before. Let God tell you something now! The body of Christ is so blasted predictable that our adversary works effortlessly. Let's hit the devil from a whole new direction. Strategize! Write down the Lord's brave new idea. Get off the well-worn path and venture out; it can help millions! Crown each sentence with scripture and see to it that it has the aroma of the impossible.

3. **Don't mingle with those who are mediocre!**

   "The righteous should choose his friends carefully..." (Proverbs 12:26). Your inner circle should be composed of positive people. When you are tired and perhaps doubtful, you need to be around positive friends, friends who challenge you to greatness. Pessimists will wear you down, and an emotional parasite will eat up your time and drain your dreams.

34

4. **Never give up!**

   All the talent, opportunity and money in the world will never compare to righteous persistence in the creation of greatness. When you fall, get up. When you fail, try again. When you're overwhelmed, keep moving. Edison failed on 1000 prototypes before he made a light bulb that worked.

5. **Forgive!**

   Why is the person who controls his spirit greater than the one who can take a city? Because inner bitterness eventually will sabotage any outward success. The forgiver gets to keep the city he has taken.

   The one who can't forgive carries past hurts, relives wrongs done to him and even comes to expect friends to fail him. This sets up more bitter experiences until he is too weighed down to move forward.

6. **Guard your greatness!**

   You are an eagle in a world of chickens. The poultry that surrounds you is threatened by your growth and courage; society is now designed to enhance the halfhearted. Study your dream; polish your vision; never take your eyes off the prize. Keep your eyes peeled for tendencies within and without that erode your pursuit of excellence.

7. **Never ripen!**

   Success wants to retire; greatness never does. Some seek a business that will be a cash cow to take care of them. The great ones can't retire while there is one villain still left at large. Stay hungry; stay excited!

Finally, my friend, understand that seeking to be great in your assigned arena is not ego but the true spark of God within you. *"By this my Father is glorified, that you bear much fruit..."* (John 15:8)

Time is running out and you are being called by the Master to rescue America from the moral black hole that is swallowing her. So I exhort, plead and beseech you: **Be great before it's too late!**

VII. THE COMING AMERICAN IRON CURTAIN

Dear Friends,

Leaders and experts I trust are confirming my greatest heartbreak: a new iron curtain is coming down over America. That ugly apparatus from Russia has been redecorated and is being slowly set up over here!

The door for preaching the gospel in America is closing!

Already the United States is the least evangelized nation of all the major nations in North and South America! More laws have been enacted that restrict preaching in the last ten years than in the previous 190 years of American history. Local governments routinely fight church expansion. The nation's largest group of lawyers has announced its plan to systematically target Christian organizations.

The most dangerous development is the radical shift in America's moral base. Family values are trampled under the worship of the all-important economy. The immorality that ruined our ability to compete and produce is not even considered! Instead, short-sighted people want government to come and rescue us again.

We are in a classic position to be hoodwinked into accepting good old-fashioned leftist socialism. *Such socialism always targets Christianity.*

Why do I recognize the symptoms so well? Because I lived in Berkeley; I saw Marxist economics in action. It bashes the church, it numbs incentive, it intellectualizes laziness.

The media and the government are in complicity to force-feed us this "new left" leftover. They manipulate statistics to justify wasteful programs. They say there are 30 million Americans living below poverty level. Paul Harvey said on radio last week, "What they don't tell you is that 40% of those they claim are in poverty actually own their own homes and their houses are twice the size of comparable Japanese workers. I am sick of this manipulation of statistics and bashing of America." Sure our economy needs help, but it *is sin that is killing us and government expansion will create a far greater monster than the recession ever was!*

I grew up on poverty. The racial slurs that were screamed at me did hurt, but what was really poisonous was the way social workers patronized us and reinforced our sense of inferiority by patting our heads and saying, "There, there, we'll take care of you!" Had Jesus not saved me, this system would have food-stamped and welfared me into a menial life.

Shame on Congress for bringing this iron curtain down upon us! First they cause the recession by pandering to so many projects like the savings and loan scandal, then they foment a corrupt and inept welfare system that fattens bureaucrats, misses the truly needy, and allows crafty deadbeats to play it like a broken slot machine. Now they want to expand their power, bounce more checks and blame others for our bad times.

Shame on the media for bringing down this iron curtain on us! They're doing exposes that stereotype ministers as crooks while airing specials that "normalize" homosexuality.'

What a pathetic set-up.

It's all so painfully familiar: "Tax the rich to pay for all our problems!" Never mind that even if we bankrupted all the wealthy, it wouldn't even make a dent in our deficit. You cannot punish people for succeeding and reward people for not trying without creating a nation of whining brats!

The Russian Revolution offered the deceived masses the narcotic of violence.   This new American socialism offers a new narcotic: instant gratification! They promise that: "We'll legitimize your sexual perversion." "We'll protect your need to use abortion as a contraceptive." "We'll pay the difference for your shabby work." And finally, "We'll get church morality off your back."

This is nothing short of the reeducation of the American mind so that we can accept the mass rejection of Christianity and a free market economy.

Examples range from the silly to the disastrous! How

can you explain unions shutting down the Saturn auto plant just as it became the first American car that was beating Japan? Why are Bibles easier to give away in Russian schools that in American schools? Why are anti-abortion protesters subjected to much more brutality than any other protesters?

Is this iron curtain inevitablel? A thousand times no! Time is short but we most certainly can still win!Based on past history, here are three good things that I am counting on to happen:

1. **The arrogant media will fall on their face!**

   These inflated moguls ooze arrogance. They are so blind that they cannot see their bias and broadcast overkill; but the public is getting sick and angry. Even when viewers agree with a liberal position, they are still angry with the media for the way they bully any opposing view.

2. **Look for a mass student rebellion!**

   As soon as students sense that Bibles are "illegal" or that Christian meetings are "off limits" they are going to overrun these philosophical walls and birth a nuclear underground church the likes of which our nation has never seen!

3. **The resurrection of the sleepy American church!**

   The drowsy disciples are finally going to cry, "enough is enough!" They will combine faith with action. Pastors and evangelists are going to discard "men pleasing" and thunder sermons that will expose this coming iron curtain! They will challenge ordinances and politicians that persecute church work and return fire on these new attacks on the Bible!

Above all we, the army of God must take the current debate and drag it kicking and screaming back to the real issue! The recession is the result of our condoning of pleasure, greed and godlessness.

America's edge has always been her Christian conscience. Discarding that has cut off our air supply! We should be asking why our cities are burning, not why interest rates are fluctuating. We should not be alarmed about jobs, so much of the loss of our national sanity.

There is a fire in my bones about this new iron curtain! It's showing in our crusades!

Thank God that we can report that crowds are swelling wherever we go. Miracles are coming like rain! We are taking our case directly to the American people!

The crisis is urgent and the vision is working. Multitudes of Americans are pressing into the Kingdom.

This gospel that we bear is the power of God to everyone! I implore you to join us in this hour of decisive action. Together let us take up the sword of the Spirit and shred this new iron curtain!

VIII. GENERATION X AND THE 30-YEAR CURSE

Dear Friends,

Strap yourself in for a jolting fact: In a 24-month span between 1962 and 1964, a conspiracy of factors destroyed or damaged every American institution. This maelstrom of evil wrought more devastation to the soul of America than the total harm of the Civil War and two subsequent world wars.

Bluntly stated, we were no longer a blessed nation, but a cursed nation. This curse has endowed us with the steepest, deadliest decline ever seen by a world power.

To be sure, Russia has fallen apart quickly, but they never knew the heights of America in blessing.

The incalculable misery and toll on our way of life can only now be told. Should we hear every social agency give a "before and after" report, here is what we would be told:

1. Before 1964, emergency rooms were manageable centers of healing. Afterwards they became nightmares of mass carnage where, now, people sit for hours with bullet wounds and no pain killer - the legacy of the drug war.

2. Before 1964, mental hospitals worked. Today they are a visit to hell where inmates overrun burned out work forces. Only a fraction of the needy can be helped in a nation that has literally lost its mind.

3. The pre-1964 record for runaways was 90,000 in one year.

Afterward it zoomed to one million youth per year and has stayed high ever since.

4. Divorce became a way of life for over half of all marriages. Today, a home where both parents are raising two children amounts to only 6% of the population.

5. Sexual abuse before 1964 was an unheard of travesty. Now, one out of six boys and one out of three girls are sexually molested.

6. Today the leading cause of death for children under five years of age is their parents.

7. Our nation's capital annually records more abortions than live births.

What happened in these 24 months of infamy? Here are four factors:

1. **John Kennedy is assassinated.**

   The baby boomers were melded by fear and uncertainty. Each of us, of this generation, remembers exactly what we are doing the moment we hears of his death.

   This man embodies an entire generation's hopes and ideals. The killing in Dallas told frightened children that no one was safe and that evil could squash good at will.

2. **The Beatles come to America.**

   Their syrupy ballads were false medication for a pain-riddled generation. Once this music went mainstream, it introduced drug use and eastern mysticism on a scale unheard of in history.

3. **Vietnam.**

   No long explanation needed here. This war, which epito-
   mized anger, despair, and futility is the only war we have
   never ended. It changed form and moved from the jungle
   to the psyche of America. Whatever ideals survived the
   death of Kennedy were summarily destroyed and the Vietnam curse continues to destroy.

4. **Prayer is banned in the public school.**

   God hears the prayers of children! Their prayer was a
   simple cry for blessing: "Lord we ask your blessing on
   our *leaders, our parents, our teachers, and ourselves.*"
   When we silenced this prayer for blessing, we remove a
   canopy of protection.

Twenty-four months is all it took for the moral immune
system of the greatest nation on Earth to be dismantled.

Perhaps the clearest consequence of the curse is Generation X - the first generation raised in America without prayer
and with boomers for parents. The post-war babies were called
the "boom generation."

These twenty-somethings are called the "bust generation."
They are accused of having no identity, no soil for greatness.
They are expected to sit out their turn at impacting America.
With them, indecision prevails. Every hairstyle is accept-
able. Clothing fads run the gamut from the 60's hip garb, to
Republican yuppie suits, to Seattle grunge. Their musical
tastes are so eclectic as to be non-descript. As many listen to
country as they do rap. They have no grand unifying theme.

They have adopted no manifesto.

Unlike the boomers that staged mass rebellion behind a congealed message, Generation X seems overwhelmed, paralyzed by future shock. They have learned to accept limits. They assume they will live in smaller homes and with less of a standard of living than their parents. They have had to downsize their dreams.

Above all, they are angry at the boomers. They accuse them of overstaying their turn in the youth culture. The "forever teenagers", they believe, used up everything and are too self-absorbed to nurture the next generation.

Before we write off Generation X as "emotionally incapable of greatness", as an expert said, let us look at an Old Testament miracle that I believe is about to be repeated in America.

Josiah became king, according to II Kings 22, when he was eight years old. He began to wrestle with his identity in his twenties.

Talk about lacking the soil for greatness! He had weeds for a family tree. His grandfather, Manassah, was the greatest mass murderer of prophets ever and his father, Ammon, was a moral sewer rat.

No one mentored Josiah. He became king because of an assassination. Yet he became the most powerful, zealous reformer in Jewish history. How could this be? The answer lies in a mysterious prophecy.

It all began when the desecrated temple in Jerusalem was

being renovated. An old book was found and it was delivered to the king.

Josiah read it, and the effect was astonishing. He tore his clothes and roared like a lion. The "Bambi eyes" he saw the world through became pilot lights, and he went into a frenzy of righteousness that drove him to cleanse an entire nation.

In fact, Josiah did more to remove witchcraft, idols, and cultural sin in the shortest span of time than any king in the Bible.

What he read that fateful day was what you and I now know as I Kings 13. But one verse exploded off the page — verse 2:

"Then he cried out against the altar by the word of the Lord and said "O altar, altar! Thus says the Lord: Behold, a child, Josiah by name, shall be born to the house of David; and on you he shall sacrifice the priests of the high places who burn incense on you, and men's bones shall be burned on you.'"

Here, Jeroboam, the architect of Israel's idolatry, was being confronted by a prophet 355 years before this young king was born. And the prophet said the name "Josiah."

An external shock wave coursed through this Generation X king. Here was the Bible speaking of his name before his birth, and more importantly, of his destiny to burn up the evil of his time!

His transformation was so complete and his reformation so mighty that these words summed up his life:

"Moreover Josiah put away those who consulted mediums and spiritists, the household gods and idols, all the abominations that were seen in the land of Judah and in Jerusalem, that he might perform the words of the law which were written in the book that Hilkiah the priest found in the house of the Lord. Now before him there was no king like him, who turned to the Lord with all his might, according to the Law of Moses; nor after him did any arise like him." (II Kings 22:24)

Generation X has no great unifying theme. Why? They have not yet seen their destiny. I am declaring here that they are chosen to reverse the curse of the last 30 years.

God, I believe, will remove the "X"! Their name is also in the book - in Isaiah 58:12:

"Those from among you shall build the old waste places; You shall raise up the foundations of many generations; And you shall be called The Repairer of the Breach, the Restorer of Streets to Dwell In."

Here is what they are destined to do in America:

1. **Build the old waste places.**

   Their environmental causes, I believe, are but shadows of their true calling - to clean and build what are presently the moral toxic waste dumps of our nation.

2. **Raise up the foundations of many generations.**

   Generation X will reconstruct concepts long lost by the curse. Equality, justice, and opportunity are distant ideas that they will bring near and raise up. They will retrieve the truths of many prior generations.

3. **Restore paths to dwell in.**

   By God's power, their impact will be felt in what are now unsafe neighborhoods. Physically and spiritually they will open up places and ways of living that have been long lost.

4. **Repair the breach.**

   The United States is divided at the soul. Racial hatred is positioning most American cities for unprecedented bloodshed.

   But our breach is not just racial. America is a breeding ground of division where formerly unimportant opinions now carry an emotional charge that can explode at any time.

   This chosen generation can wade in and defuse our hatred with prophetic power.

   Generation X is like Josiah, a moral miracle waiting to happen! Let all preachers be warned: *Get in your pulpit and zero in on your "twenty-somethings."* They are marked and will be set aflame by preaching on *destiny.*

   Our obedience will transform them from orphans, adrift and bewildered, to focused prophetic warriors.

   Is God finished with America? Just the opposite! He has just begun to fight!

   Go to prayer and listen. Soon you will hear the distant rumble of a locomotive. They are coming this way, a generation who cannot be stopped because they have found their place in prophecy.

IX. WET DYNAMITE

Dear Friends,

It was a bomb waiting to go off! We should not have been shocked by the L.A. riots. For years, anger and injustice had been building up. The Central Los Angeles gangs planned some sort of mayhem all along and Rodney King provided the fuse they were waiting for.

The church also waits to explode but it's amazing, however, how little real clout the Christian church has in America. Preachers have little or no impact on the secular mind.

We can't swallow this fact. We have built buildings like never before. We have attached the air waves and seemed to gain footholds on many fronts. Yet here we sit in large numbers, strong in resources, seemingly organized, with an unprecedented opportunity in America, but there is no spiritual explosion. Has there ever been a more over-prepared, totally equipped army than the current generation of American Christians? By all rights, we should have had a national revival by now. This is a baffling moment. You can justify two completely opposite pictures of America. You can say we are morally at an all-time low, and you can just as easily observe that churches are growing everywhere.

According to Gallup, there are an estimated 70 million born-again Christians in the United States. But how could this be? How could we be so grossly pagan from coast to coast and have that many claiming to know Jesus? You must

49

either say that this is an extremely exaggerated number or there is something horrendously wrong with many of who claim Christ. To say there aren't that many of us out there is easy. To say America is hopeless and marked for judgment is easy. You just give into the despair of the day.

While I am sure there is some exaggeration, there remains the fact that this estimate of how many Christians are in America did not come from an evangelist; it came from the secular press. So the problem must lie mainly in the individual condition of believers in our country.

We have an epidemic of uncommitted Christians. It is as simple as that. Most responded to appeals but their repentance does not cause a revolution in their behavior. While most are afraid to reject Christ, they are equally reluctant to follow Christ into victorious faith. The result is a generation that believes in Jesus Christ but does not follow Him to battle.

Napoleon said an army travels on its stomach. However, the army of God travels on its heart. The heart for war is in only a handful of believers today. These "nominals" cannot see the utter viciousness of evil and the ferocious zeal of God to attack it. We have the greatest explosion potential ever but our dynamite is wet.

If the church cannot get on fire, no wonder our nation has lost her moral compass. Take a careful look at us. We are a generation preoccupied with escapism, drowning in trivial pursuits.

Preachers are supposed to attack this and release people

into authentic life in Christ. Instead, many pulpits cater to it. This theology asks God to engage a bratty child in whims. Vast numbers of preachers have portrayed faith as painless and profitable. So now we have reaped a generation that can't stand in adversity and refuses to grow. Probably the most abused phrase today is, *"God loves you just the way you are."* Let me assure you that I believe it is true, but the way it has been applied is "I don't need to change; I don't have to grow up." *God loves us too much to leave us the way we are.*

Nowhere is this more painfully clear that in the priorities of believers. Recently, American Christians were asked which they would rather have, teaching on controlling their feelings of depression or training to win souls. The vast majority want the therapy. This means we are so in need of confidence and self-esteem that there is nothing left over for winning America.

How can you have revival when a generation of Christians is turned inward instead of giving out? Some have even tried to negotiate a truce between two attitudes of living that are totally opposed to each other — God and mammon. Too many preachers have become investment counselors. True preachers who are called to preach to you are not here to furnish your living room, but to equip your living soul to face life squarely and triumphantly.

We have all the resources we need to revive America, but we don't have enough of the central element: believers whose walk with God has teeth. We must have more than amusement park faith. We must have the type of faith that forces demons to let go of a nation that is born of God. Our choice is clear. Either we become God-anointed vessels or we lose America. We cannot draw false comfort from the fact that nearly 70 million Americans claim to be born again.

All is not bleak, however. The church now has a growing appetite to become armed and dangerous. After stumbling and falling in a pseudo-discipleship many are wanting a genuine fire power. They are sick of hearing about formulas that sound good in meetings but don't have authority against real-life problems and the powers of darkness.

I refuse to stew over all the immature Christians. I'd rather seize this historic moment and fan their embers of faith into raging fires of revival.

The explosion is about to come, but key steps must be taken right now to dry out the dynamite! Here are the steps I believe we must take now:

1. The leadership of the church must alter its messages **to produce disciples who want to conquer the present evil, not just survive it.** We must teach love and acceptance hand in hand with a commission to perform exploits for God.

2. **We must slay the dragon of our fears.** We cannot wallow in the same pity party as the world. To be Christian is to renounce pessimism about tomorrow and say with our actions that we have received a kingdom that cannot be shaken. "....*Let* us have grace by which we may serve God acceptably with reverence and godly fear." (Hebrews

12:28)

Let the world gorge every last morsel of a dying age. Our destination is a city not made with hands whose builder and maker is God. We do not need a vast reward or a vain show of materialism here.

"This I say, therefore, and testify in the Lord, that you should no longer walk as the rest of the Gentiles walk, in the futility of their mind." (Ephesians 4:17)

Jesus in us means we can be bold, be joyous, be supernatural and give true bread and living water to all who ask.

3. We must develop rage toward evil. "Then the spirit of God came upon Saul when he heard this news, and his anger was greatly aroused." (I Samuel 11:6)

The fear of the Lord is to hate evil..." (Proverbs 8:13)

The world is filled with hate but it is the wrong kind of hate, of brother against brother. The hatred I refer to is a righteous indignation toward Satan. David's arms were once strong enough to bend a bow of bronze, but when he lost his heart for war they became limp and weak, and he fell into sin with Bathsheba.

A simple New Year's resolution will not do. A person must first hate the tricks Satan has played on him to keep him powerless. He must then hate the kind of person he has allowed himself to become. After this, he is ready for a heart for war and to truly hate what God hates. Out of this will emerge power for daily living.

4. **Turn away from teaching that condones sin.** "For certain men have crept in unnoticed, who long ago were marked out for this condemnation, ungodly men, who turn the grace of our God into lewdness and deny the only Lord God and our **Lord** *Jesus Christ.*" (Jude 4, NIV)

Do not abuse the grace of God. Make a commitment to grow. Yes, God is merciful and forgiving, but His grace is not a license to stay in sin. Thank God we have rediscovered His love and His goodness, but love means that He wants to cleanse us and make us new. God gives strength to those sincerely seeking health and He does not condemn.

"Seeing then that we have a great High Priest who has passed through the heavens, Jesus the Son of God, let us hold fast our confession. For we do not have a High Priest who cannot sympathize with our weaknesses, but was in all points tempted as we are, yet without sin." (Hebrews 4:15-16)

5. **God will give you something to do - do it.** All dealings of God become action. The Spirit of God will get you involved somewhere. The only way you will ever know that you have gone from surviving to being triumphant in Christ is when you have started to minister to someone else. It is time for you to get alone and pray wholeheartedly to be useful. Talent is not the major issue. Commitment is. A powerful door of opportunity will open to anyone who is serious about being involved.

We must take action now to see the explosion of God that we should have seen long ago. And let me assure you, the explosion **is** coming. Though many stumble in the dark now, they will come into the destined greatness of the army of God.

Christians are ready to hear the message. The new cry of believers in the United States is "Give me something great to do for God!" A mass explosion is inevitable!

X. PROPHETS OR PRIMA DONNAS?

Dear Friends,

The five-year period from 1947 to 1952 saw one of history's most significant expressions of power. Many great men and women of God - such as Billy Graham, Oral Roberts and Kathryn Kuhlman - were raised up and mightily used by the Lord.

But the roar of spiritual giants is not in the land today. There is a glaring spiritual void which exists in America. There is an absence of true apostles, prophets, evangelists, pastors and teachers. We need leaders who are not in ministry for the money, the power, the public attention or the acclaim, but leaders who truly hear from God.

How can Bible schools instruct their students how to pull the trigger of God's power on this generation when the teachers themselves don't know how? The word "sacrifice" has been dropped from the vocabulary of leadership and laity alike. Even in many Charismatic quarters, the concept of "dying to self" has been replaced by an emphasis on being "King's kids" who are entitled to power and wealth. We are not even thinking about defeating the devil or changing America.

The devil is not threatened by men who have the ability to speak eloquently. The only thing that terrifies him is the work of the Cross of Christ in a man or a woman's life. Those who have paid the price - who are not in ministry for fame or glory or self-enrichment, but who desire to be used by God - strike fear in Satan's heart.

It is inevitable in today's atmosphere for prima donna preachers to rise up.

I Kings 1:6 says David had not rebuked Adonijah at any time with the question, "Why have you done this?" Adonijah had been spoiled by his father. We, too, have our own generation of spoiled sons who have been led to believe that God will grant them whatever they request, whenever they ask for it!

"Now King David was old and stricken in years; and they covered him with clothes, but he gat no heat ... Then Adonijah, the son of Haggith exalted himself, saying, I will be king ..." (I Kings 1:1, 5 KJV). Adonijahs will arise whenever people perceive the authority of aging Davids to be silent or ineffective.

On the surface, it must have seemed to Israel that David was no longer competent.

The Davids of this past generation - the anointed, mighty men of God - were old. Adonijahs, (self-proclaimed leaders), proclaim themselves king. God has neither raised them up nor ordained them, but they have taken advantage of the advancing age of the Davids and the powerful 40-year period of spiritual giants in our land. The Adonijahs declare themselves called of God when they are not; they sell their books and tapes; they say they have visions when they do not.

While there are a host of mighty young prophets, there

are also many so-called teachers infecting the Church with spiritual instantism: an overnight, quick-fix, full-grown, microwaved Christianity that claims to make spiritual giants overnight. And you can get-rich-quick besides!

How dare we conduct gospel ministry as if it were a New York stock exchange! Many Adonijahs cannot even hear the Lord's agenda: "I want you to rid yourself of lust, greed, pride, and arrogance. I want you to get right with Me. I want you to love the lost."

When miracles are not active in the Church, Adonijahs will surface. Many will follow them for a season. If one looks closely, our Adonijahs can be easily spotted. Without marketing and promotion, they have no flavor, no vitality, no compelling message and no solution to the evil of the day.

"Then Adonijah ... exalted himself, saying, I will be king: and he prepared for himself chariots and horsemen, and fifty men to run before him" (I Kings 1:5). He had the appearance of a king; he rented some kingly-looking horses; he had learned to market himself as a king.

Adonijahs, have style without substance. But their ministries are made of the most flammable substance known as hype.

Yet these Adonijahs are considered by many Christians to be "the men of the hour." But where are the people who were converted through their ministries? If we counted all the Americans who were "saved" in the last decade through these Adonijahs, the results would be staggering. America in its entirety would have been saved three times over! Yet abortion is still a reality, drugs are still rampant, and morality continues to fall.

Adonijah made a fatal mistake in overlooking the heart of King David. Adonijah did not realize a man consists of his spiritual make-up - not of his physical constitution. I Kings 1 says Bathsheba and the prophet Nathan entered David's chamber and informed him that the kingdom was in trouble. Resting on one elbow, David barked orders like the young boy who had killed the giant, who had governed over the mighty men, who had struck fear and terror in all the kingdoms of the world. "Then King David answered and said, 'Call me Bathsheba'. And she came into the king's presence ... And the king sware, and said ... Assuredly Solomon thy son shall reign after me, and he shall sit upon my throne in my stead; even so I will certainly do this day ... let Zadok the priest, and Nathan the prophet anoint him there king over Israel ..." (I Kings 1:28-30, 34).

A lot of arrogant young preachers presume they are Holy Ghost big shots because they've led a few souls to Christ, sold some tapes, and received some fame and publicity. But the older generation has seen the fire and the glory of God. They know the true miracles of Christ. They are more readily able to discern the difference between gold and fool's gold, the anointing and emotion, and between self-promotion and God-given favor.

Too often a minister's success is gauged by his popularity or by the size of his ministry's budget. David's greatness was that he repeatedly and voluntarily placed his life on the line for the sake of truth. Godless, carnal experts advise today's preachers. But no risk, no courage, no vision and no power are in it. Older leaders must slay this "life insurance" mentality.

Retirement is not an option for a man with God's hand on him. He needs to have an iron will which says, "Whenever the need arises - whenever the devil rears his ugly head — I'm ready to spring from my bed and be a lion for God."

Last year Vic Munyer, who was like a father to me, went to be with Jesus. He had been an usher for Billy Graham Crusades since 1948. In spite of his chronological age, he was younger than I am. The secret of his youth was that he refused to talk about previous moves of God. He was constantly rising up and was always available when the kingdom needed him.

After Solomon's coronation, a release occurred in the nation of Israel. "...All the people came up after him (Solomon), and the people piped with pipes, and rejoiced with great joy, so that the earth rent with the sound of them." (I Kings 1:40). Previously, the people had so fervently wanted a king, they accepted the prospect of Adonijah as their new ruler. But it was not a wholehearted, enthusiastic acceptance.

On the other hand, when Solomon was announced as King David's successor, the cry from the people of God was so deafening that it tore the ground upon which they stood.

The prophetic had conquered the prima donna!

Older, established ministries will either ride on the new wave or fade into monumental nostalgia and speak of days gone by. The leaders can look for a Charismatic rest home or they can get up on their elbows and say, "I will be on a fire as long as I am on this earth! I will be a part of everything God is doing!" We still need our Davids to give balance, direction and force.

A person called to be a Solomon would never indulge self-promotion. Proverbs 18:16 states that a man's gift will make room for him and establish him. "... Promotion cometh neither from the east, nor from the west, nor from the south. But God ... putteth down one, and setteth up another." (Psa. 75:6,7)

To Solomon, the Lord said, "... If thou wilt walk before me, as David thy father walked, in integrity of heart, and in uprightness, to do according to all that I have commanded thee, and wilt keep my statutes and my judgments: Then I will establish the throne of thy kingdom upon Israel forever ..." (I Kings 9:4,5). God's blessing is reserved for those committed to walking according to His Word.

How sad that so many settle for the morsels of human-powered religious entertainment. It is high time for some Holy Ghost untouchables whose words do not fall to the ground but pierce the darkness!

XI. GOD DIDN'T WAKE ME UP TO ASK YOU FOR MONEY!

Dear Friends,

Because a shameful practice has become widespread, this letter must be written. Ministries have been duped into fundraising tactics and letters that border on pure fraud.

For example, let's look first at a personalized letter that begins with the words, "Dear Mario Murillo, ...Last night God woke me up and brought your name before me." The letter will go on and describe how important and special I am to this person. Soon the letter will tell me about a special blessing God has for me and before it is over, a connection will be made between this blessing and my donation to the ministry of the writer. Whenever a letter like this is sent, three very serious sins are committed.

1. **The first sin is a telling a lie.** You and I both know that the only one who woke up was the computer that is programmed to put your name and mine in just the right places so that the letter looks personalized. Because these mailings are sent out by the thousands, we know that God did not wake up the minister thousands of times and pass all the names of his donors before him individually. I know it is a serious charge, but you can't get around it: he's lying, or he had one of the worst nights in history.

    If the minister is lying, this raises serious questions about his character. Is he also lying when he is in the pulpit? Is he lying about what he does with your money? Is he telling you that he doesn't think you are very intelligent? Does he actually believe that you will be convinced that he sat down and wrote a personal letter to you?

2. **They say God spoke, thereby misrepresenting the Lord.** This the scripture denounces most adamantly.

   "They have envisioned futility and false divination, saying, ''Thus says the Lord!' But the Lord has not sent them; yet they hope that the word may be confirmed. "Have you not seen a futile vision, and have you not spoken false devination? You say, 'The Lord says,' but I have not spoken." Therefore thus says the Lord God: "Because you have spoken nonsense and envisioned lies, therefore I am indeed against you," says the Lord God. "My hand will be against the prophets who envision futility and who devine lies; they shall not be in the assembly of My people, nor be written in the record of the house of Israel, nor shall they enter into the land of Israel. Then you shall know that I am the Lord God. " (Ezekiel 13:6-9)

   "God told me" are the three most frightening words a preacher will ever utter. Yet these words are indiscriminately attached to pet projects of men as a means of extracting funds from the faithful. The Bible calls it false prophecy.

3. **The third sin may be the most dangerous, that of creating an image of God's character that is completely**

false. It is blasphemous to imagine our great and mighty God in this scenario: "Hey, wake up! I'm giving you the name of a person on your mailing list. He has a serious need but there is no way I'm going to help him until he gives you money." This flies in the face of everything the gospel stands for.

"He who did not spare His own Son, but delivered Him up for us all, how shall He not with Him also freely give us all things?" (Romans 8:32)

"Buying a blessing" is a terrible abuse of scripture. To promise healing in exchange for a donation is as low as a preacher will ever stoop in fundraising. Yet this is the very thing that happens again and again in Christian fundraising.

In a recent televised appeal for money, a well-known evangelist who was trying to buy back property "Satan had stolen" turned to a guest pastor and said, "Pastor, I believe you have a word from God." The pastor pointed directly into the camera and started "talking to" a women with severe stomach cancer. The minister said clearly, "If you will be obedient and give that $500 you know God wants you to give, you will be healed!"

In the Old Testament the judgment of the Lord was directed toward anyone who tried to profit from the miracles of God. (See II Kings 5:21-27) As you read this letter, you will see that Gehazi, the servant of Elijah, accepted gifts from Naaman who had just been healed of leprosy. God cursed Gehazi with the leprosy of Naaman.

64

Daniel ordered King Belshazzar to give his gifts to someone else after Daniel gave the king God's word.

"Then Daniel answered, and said before the king, "Let your gifts be for yourself, and give your rewards to another; yet I will read the writing to the king, and make known to him the interpretation." (Daniel 5:17)

How can we face God, who gave Jesus to be beaten and die for our salvation and healing, and imply that any further payment is due in order to receive from God.

These three sins are so blatant that we cannot take an apathetic attitude. These repugnant practices should not be tolerated any longer! This is what I suggest you do if you are receiving fundraising letters of this kind.

1. Mail them a wake-up call. Write to them and tell them that they are offending you. Good ministries will repent and clean up their appeals. You are not being judgemental or negative; on the contrary, you are part of the error yourself if you don't speak up against this flagrant abuse in fundraising.

2. If they don't repent, get off their mailing list and stop sending them money. The only way some will stop is if it hurts them financially. More importantly, if they are phony, then we had better not support them anyway.

   Remember, these fundraising tactics are a grievous offense to God and they bring shame to the gospel.

3. Search your own heart as to why you give. One important reason that ministries have resorted to these tactics is

that Christians have become carnal in their giving. American culture is on the take and that cultural sin is now in the church. Too many of us only give to get back. Many ministries feel pressured to compete for the limited donor dollars that are out there and consultants deceive them by telling them that selfishness is the approach that works right now. Let me reaffirm that giving does reap a return! My point is that our heart must be generous not greedy.

Here are two nasty habits that have crept in to the giver:

ONE: <u>Giving to receive instead of out of love and gratitude to God</u>. Consider the woman I mentioned earlier who was told to give $500 in order to receive healing for stomach cancer. If she believes she can buy healing, she is acutally prolonging her sickness by hurting God with a bribe. God heals out of mercy. Our giving must only be done out of worship and a sincere love for the lost.

TWO: <u>Giving sporadically.</u> Giving must become a consistent habit of Christian living. When we are constantly bombarded with hype, we can become dull to the Spirit's prodding. Many ministries use crisis and the spectacular to awaken our senses. True disciples don't need this form of stimulation because they have made giving a regular part of their lives. Their hearts are sensitive to the Holy Spirit and they prayerfully examine the ministries they support.

I give regularly and choose carefully where I give. If I get a stream of crisis letters, I start to wonder how well that ministry manages their resources. There is no excuse for many ministries resorting to questionable fundraising tactics, even though we can see why there is pressure on leaders. People have become fickle and often leave the work of God in jeopardy.

The most important choice I ever made in ministry was to stand in faith when financial pressure strikes the ministry. The backbone of Mario Murillo Ministries is not the occasional big gift but that wonderful disciple who does something eachmonth because he loves God and obeys His voice.

God did not wake me up last night and tell me to ask you for money. I trust Him to wake YOU up and confirm to your heart how vital our work for Christ is.

I want to close with our philosophy of fundraising. These are truths that have kept Mario Murillo Ministries from danger. I recommend them to all ministries.

1. Keep ego out of your projects. "Do nothing out of selfish ambition or vain conceit ..." (Philippians 2:3)
   Often ministers are tempted to take on projects that are man-made, not ordered of God. Styles and trends should never dictate success to us; only obedience is success. If God didn't tell you to do it or build it, remember, you, my friend, not God, will have to pay for it.

2. Pray before you write an appeal letter. There may be sin

or disobedience in you or your ministry that has dried up funds. You may need to repent instead of rushing to the people for more money. Ask God for directions to know how to restore His blessing. When you write honest letters on behalf of an honest need, God will speak to the people to give to your ministry.

3. <u>Make soul winning and helping the oppressed your prime directive.</u> God's heart is to get the gospel to those whom Satan oppresses; He has no other pet project! If you live to expand the kingdom of God, you will be founded on a rock.

4. <u>Put the money where you say you're going to put it</u>. No single abuse has brought more people down than misappropriation of money. If it is for starving children, take nothing out; send it all! If you have a fund set aside for a godly project, do not spend it on anything else. We live in desperate times and there is no room for carnality in the work of God today.

I believe God is signaling us all that He will no longer tolerate financial abuse. You must choose wisely whom you will support, why you support, and how you support the work of God.

XII. IN SEARCH OF ELIJAH'S BODY

Dear Friends,

Admittedly, this is an odd title. However, it addresses an odd problem.

Right now you and I both know believers who are excited and those who are bored. Some have a sense that something awesome will soon happen while others stiffen with dread at any mention of the future.

Many who used to charge into church filled with anticipation now battle to stay awake through an entire service. Their passion for Christ is gone and one reason is that we are searching for Elijah's body.

Before I explain, let me ask you ... w*hat makes a Christian excited?* First is the appreciation of the new life we have found; then the pure adventure of following Jesus. These two elements are usually present in new converts. The problem arises when they begin to interact with deadwood in the church. These mummies will see to it that the young and adventurous lose their excitement and fade into religious habit.

Here is where we so often err: we associate excitement with being new to Christ. We falsely assume that the excitement will cool off and we don't realize that a great part of the thrill is being a part of what *God is doing at this time in history.*

After the euphoria of being born again subsides, the excitement of living out God's plan should take over. Look at any bored believer and you'll see a tarnished vision and a muddled lack of purpose.

Let me dispel a popular notion. Churches do not grow and thrive because of the finebuilding, the fair-haired pastor, or the seemingly complete program. The real reason for growth today is clear!

Growth occurs when you mingle timeless truths with a revelation of the timely acts of God. Bluntly stated, churches grow where something is going on! That something is a visitation of God. Excited believers are created by being involved in what God is doing now.

You and I both know churches that seemingly have every good component known to man and angel, yet without success. This is now more true than ever because we are seeing a major changing of the guard. The entire landscape of the Holy Ghost movement is being altered.

The Book of Second Kings, chapter two, records a similar point of change. Elijah made his fiery exit and Elisha took up his mantle. Elijah's groupies were standing on the other side of the river waiting for their hero to return as he had always done in the past.

The new prophet Elisha appeared, raised the mantle, and struck the waters. The waters parted as they had for the old prophet. The river made no distinction between Elijah and Elisha; the river knew the anointing of God. The groupies were another matter; they wanted Elijah, not God's purposes.

Elisha asked them, "Where is the God of Elijah?" This

question cut to the heart of that generation's problem. They had their designated prophet and they begged Elisha to let them go to look for Elijah's body. They suspected that the Spirit had dropped Elijah on a mountain.

How ridiculous to go looking for a memory when God has deposited the future right into your hand. This describes the last ten years of the Pentecostal/Charismatic movement. We elevated men until they could do no wrong; we even over-looked their glaring flaws. One pastor said to me, "We were so shocked when these legends self-destructed, even though they had been acting bizarre for years!"

Today there are many fresh, young voices. But there is a hideous double standard! We will accept the Elijahs, warts and all, to their destruction while we refuse to acknowledge the most promising young voices.

Many young evangelists are discouraged by the fact that even before they get to resist the attacks of Satan, they must first survive the church. Mighty gifts and callings are being delayed because we want time to search for Elijah's body.

This generation is covered with memorabilia and para-phernalia of an age that God says is over. The final victims will be those trapped in this time warp. They will miss the great times of power just ahead.

Imagine being sidelined by nostalgia as a storm of miracles refreshes America. Our first loyalty must be to what Jesus is doing in our day. That means adapting to new names and faces.

If pastors succumb to the carnal tendency to go for what was a big name in the 80's just to draw a crowd, they run the risk of a dead meeting!

The wise person of God will discern the times. The river has parted again and we are to acknowledge where the God of Elijah is.

Many churches and ministries start out as places of power, then evolve into museums and end up as prison houses. Altars of fire become artifacts, miracles become methods, and people end up powerless.

The point is clear. We must find the mantle, not the body, of the prophet. We are not to seek Elijah; we are to seek Elijah's God.

XIII. WHY DO WE LET THEM DESTROY MARRIAGES AND CHURCHES?

"For of this sort are those who creep into households and make captives of gullible women loaded down with sins, led away by various lusts, always learning and never able to come to the knowledge of the truth." (*II Timothy 3:6-7*)

Dear Friends,

This is no witchhunt. This is no slam on women in leadership. On the contrary, this is a call for women leaders and a plea to stop widespread disaster.

The deception I target in this letter is so pervasive that I can make this chilling claim: <u>Every pastor I know has been attacked at one time or another by a Jezebel "prophet"</u> one who seeps in and controls weak sheep. Left unchecked, these Jezebels can become the leading cause of divorce among Charismatics.

What is "a Jezebel spirit"? I Kings 21:25 says: "But there was no one like Ahab who sold himself to do wickedness in the sight of the Lord, because Jezebel his wife stirred him up." Ahab did not rule by direct legitimate authority. This spirit builds control through progressive flattery, manipulation, guilt and derision. A low-grade version of the Jezebel spirit takes the form of packs of people who roam churches and pounce on a person struggling in their marriage. They tantalize them with the idea of freedom. They ask them,

"Why do you put up with them?" Finally, they become a support group during the divorce.

But this article is about the real Jezebels that Jesus warned would ravage the church in the last days.

These "prophet intercessors" can cast a compelling first impression. Some are sweet. Some pray for hours daily (which they tout like a license to minister). Often they have an entourage that float around fussing over their wonderful "gift."

Do not be fooled. Jezebel is a destroyer and can literally become God's voice to their victims. Here is how they gain control.

- First, by offering to pray with their prey. "Let me help you since your husband is so busy." They are careful not to criticize a husband or pastor.

- Jezebels lavish attention, praise, gifts, and the promise of spiritual victory on their target. Subtly the goal shifts from healing marriage to a promised "intimacy with Jesus."

- The victim becomes addicted to Jezebel's approval and is infected with a critical attitude toward her husband or pastor. This raises the tension in the marriage and leads to confrontation.

- Victims choose to follow Jezebel and breaks relationship with husband or pastor. Jezebels are rarely confronted because leaders are reluctant to challenge this complex spirit. Even Elijah ran away! Jesus not only predicted this demonic activity, He also rebuked leaders for their reluctance to expose it. Revelation 2:20-22 tells us: "Nevertheless I have a few things against you, because you allow that woman Jezebel, who calls herself prophetess, to teach and seduce My servants to commit sexual immorality and eat things sacrificed to idols."

It is easy to be accused of being against women in this present feminist environment. In reality, exposing Jezebel is very pro-woman because Jezebel is an anti-woman as one can get! Here's why:

1. Jezebel almost exclusively destroys women.

2. Jezebel reinforces the lie that competent women hate most; that is, that a female must lie, cheat, and manipulate to gain authority.

3. Jezebel hates true women of God who have come by their leadership honestly.

But know this also: Men can be Jezebels. They resemble Absalom. They lend an ear to the malcontents in a church and constantly drop hints of how much better the church would be if they were in leadership. Soon they create a congregation within a congregation that rises up against the pastor.

In San Jose, California an "intercessor," whom I will call Lori, insinuated herself into the life of a well-known preacher and his wife by claiming God sent her to help their marriage. In the process, the wife became enamored with what she believed to be a breakthrough in her walk with God. Soon it became apparent that the marital crisis was not being addressed. Instead the wife was spending an inordinate amount of time with Lori "getting words from the Lord".

The ultimate collision came when Lori gave the wife a series of "words" that encouraged the wife to retain an attorney, to separate from her husband, and go after all of their personal assets.

Lori justified this to the wife by saying that all of this destruction would make the woman's husband a better man of God. Moreover, she ordered the wife not to communicate with her husband and to refuse the counsel of highly respected pastors.

1. All Christians must be on the alert. Is someone trying to control you or a loved one? Jezebel must not go unchallenged! Leaders must take action when they see abuses at work among the sheep.

2. Promote true women leaders, they are out best defense against the Jezebel spirit. The answer to false women leaders is not dominating males, but true women of God!

3. Husbands pray with your wives. Love her, cherish her and seek to be her spiritual companion. If she would rather pray with another woman than you, your marriage is in crisis.

Remember that the real purpose of Jezebel is to divide churches, destroy marriages, and prevent women of God from assuming their rightful place in the end-time revival.

XIV. SUPERNATURAL PEACE FOR TODAY'S SUPERNATURAL STRESS

Dear Friends,

No, you are not going crazy; your life *has* gotten intense. Even simple tasks seem to possess the power to drain the life out of us. Modern life presses us on every level. There is a ferocity to even average days that can debilitate us.

Why does it seem that our body and mind are under continual attack? Why do we feel a dreadful exhaustion at the end of our days?

The sooner you realize what you are really up against, the sooner you will find relief. You live in a day of dissipation. The dictionary defined dissipation as "being spread thin to the point of vanishing".

America is at the vanishing point. A hideous monster is at large. The well-to-do feel it as severe meaninglessness that trivializes all their achievements. The middle-class feel it as crushing pressure that has no resting place. They rush faster and fall further behind.

In the impoverished inner city, it is a killer despair that foments wretched lives and unspeakable violence.

How did life get so crazy? America was deceived; America became addicted.

Back in 1964, a man could work 40 hours a week and with his pay buy a house and raise four children. The futurists predicted shorter work weeks and a life of increased leisure; what they never figured on was the dragon of materialism.

Mothers went out to get careers that would "supplement" the family income. That luxury quickly became a necessity. We started working more and more for what we had to have. Prices zoomed upward and now most mothers couldn't go home even if they wanted to. The single-income family is almost nonexistent.

The future is here and it is ugly. The average American worker now works 60 hours a week. Our stress level is vicious. Our youth are locked in a prison of possessions that has classmates killing each other for designer sneakers and label clothes.

The family unit is a war zone. We have bred a generation of "latch key children" orphaned by parents who are "doing time" for the American economy. Some even have the gall to throw scraps of attention to their children and call it "quality time."No wonder abortion is pandemic.

No wonder the inner city is a concentration camp of despair.

In the middle of all this we try to live for God. This is why we must have a militant peace Militancy and peace appear to be opposites, so how can we have a militant peace? The fabric of life now demands a kind of peace that we have not known. This kind of peace is not natural peace and it does not just happen.

Natural peace is good for natural stress. What we face

today is supernatural stress that must be answered by supernatural peace. Natural peace comes from moods and feelings that we try to create. It is circumstantially based; for normal peace to happen, things have to go right.

This is the stuff we associate with babbling brooks and colorful sunsets. So, who has the time? Worse yet, those old cures cannot dispel this new strain of stress. You can stare at fish, play classical music, use biofeedback, and it will not even dent this malignant intensity.

Satan has turned up the heat. He is pressing the attack because his time is short. *"He is filled with fury, because he knows that his time is short."* (Revelation 12:12b NIV) This great wrath on society is his final barrage to unleash misery as we have never seen it before.

We have never really had to differentiate between natural peace and God's peace but now we must. Only the peace of God is effective against today's viciousness. We must admit that we have relied on our own powers of relaxation. Now we cannot live by anything but the peace of God.

Only the peace that He gives can sustain us in our world where sudden change can instantly obliterate our human security. We have to be militant about this! This supernatural calming doesn't just happen; we must contend for it.

Our schedules don't permit us run off to a quiet creek. We aren't able to predict when an attack might come. Peace of mind is now a matter of war.

So, then, what is the prescription for a militant peace?

1. **Make a personal declaration!**

   "He who does not love Me does not keep my words; and the word which you hear is not Mine but the Father's who sent Me." (John 14:24 NIV)

   Make this personal declaration: "For the sake of those I love and for the sake of God's purposes in me and because of the onslaught of Satan, I must seek with all my heart to possess a militant peace."

   We must seek God's peace with an undivided heart. Daniel had no warning of the terrorizing experience of being thrown into the lions' den, yet he was ready. He properly discerned that life in Babylon meant his prayer life must be on red alert.

   The peace that passes understanding enveloped Daniel. Militant peace emanated from him. This awesome air of authority paralyzed the cats and they knew this man was not dinner.

   Likewise, Satan will wither and flee from you when you are clothed in godly tranquillity.

   Don't play games! God knows if you really want this peace. Burn the bridges back to your old lack of self-sufficiency. Readily agree to God's analysis of your problem and wait with an undivided heart for this supernatural peace.

2. **Realize that Jesus doesn't just give us peace. He is our peace.**

   Every great truth starts at the cross. On this visit, we

will see the special peace that Jesus won. "For He Himself is our peace, who has broken down the middle wall of separation having abolished in His flesh the enmity, that is, the law of commandments contained in ordinances, so as to create Himself one new man from the two, thus making peace, and that he might reconcile them both to God in one body through the cross, thereby putting to death the enmity." (Ephesians 2:14-16 NIV)

To begin with, He satisfied the justice of God, Making peace for the wrath created by man's fall.

To Satan, he leveled a crushing defeat that rendered Him powerless before the peace of God. By doing this, Jesus became our peace. He himself is the peace of God in us. All the power of the universe is abiding in us.

The very same voice that stilled the violent storm can rise in you to answer the insane chaos that life throws at us.

Showing that He is your peace, and letting Him function as your peace, are universes apart. Paul gave us the key in these words: "I have been crucified with Christ; it is no longer I who live, but Christ lives in me; and the *life* which I now live in the flesh I live by faith in the Son of God, who loved me and gave Himself for me." (Galatians 2:20 NIV)

The cross must do something to me. It is my turn for a resurrection but I cannot hope for a resurrection to happen without dying to self.

81

Today is a day where self-sufficiency is out greatest enemy. The flesh will do anything it can to avoid the cross. But we risk everything if our faith is fueled by human power.

We must go down into a grave where our life becomes a singlr, uninterrupted "yes" to God. Then He will raise us up. He will be our peace. When attacks come, He will react through us. We will see responses to crisis we never thought possible. We will sense a rock solid confidence that we will know is straight from heaven.

3. **Learn the daily discipline of enforcing the peace of God**.

"Be anxious for nothing, but in everything by prayer and supplication, with thanksgiving, let your requests be made known to God; and the peace of God, which surpasses all understanding, will guard your hearts and minds through Christ Jesus." (Philippians 4:6,7 NIV)

Even after a mighty work of death and resurrection, our hearts must learn to guard what God has done. We must be intensely protective of the peace of God and strive to let Him do His work daily.

Drown all issues of your life in prayer. Do it the moment they arrive. Prayer is your act of giving circumstances to God.

You are not too busy to pray anymore than you are too busy to breathe.

Why? Because prayer creates more time than it uses!

Through prayer, the hidden thieves that steal hours of our day are exposed and we are released to an effective day. Instead of confessing, "I have no time to pray," say instead, "I must pray because I have no time".

The promise is, if you do it, the peace that passes understanding will guard your heart!

There is great danger in casual living. For the indifferent, the future is certain disaster. To the discerning, there is a vast hope, a rock of salvation. Make these truths your own; move toward a militant peace. You will look and wonder at the hand of God as He neutralizes every storm Satan tries to throw at you.

XV. WHAT TO DO WHEN SATAN STEALS YOUR MIRACLE

Dear Friends,

We are never warned enough . Miracles can be *stolen!* We are often subject to vicious attacks right after God does a great miracle for us.

Scripture is replete with examples of how Lucifer attacks. In Revelation 12:4 Satan is portrayed as the dragon who sat poised to devour the child as soon as it was born. Matthew 13:4 describes the birds who swoop down on the freshly scattered seed.

The devil capitalizes on our elation over what Jesus has just done for us. We simply don't expect an attack right after victory.

These shock raids are a favorite of the enemy for a greater reason than the element of surprise. He knows that stealing a fresh act of God can stun the child of God into anger and confusion about God's character.

In first aid you learn that you must respond to a wound quickly and correctly. Spiritually you must act immediately and properly or you will allow irreparable damage to happen.

This is a warning about all miracles whether it is a healing God gave you, a breakthrough in business or marriage, a triumph over emotions or habits and especially, newfound faith in Christ.

What do we do? Can we take back what the devil has taken?

Let's begin by looking at II Kings 4:8-20:

"One day Elisha went to Shunem. And a well-to-do woman was there, who urged him to stay for a meal. So whenever he came by, he stopped there to eat. "She said to her husband, 'I know that this man who often comes our way is a holy man of God.'

"Let's make a small room on the roof and put in it a bed and a table, a chair and a lamp for him. Then he can stay there whenever he comes to us.'

"One day when Elisha came, he went up to his room and lay down there.

"He said to his servant Gehazi, 'Call the Shunammite.' So he called her, and she stood before him.

"Elisha said to him, 'Tell her, "You have gone to all this trouble for us. Now what can be done for you? Can we speak on your behalf to the king or the commander of the army?"' She replied 'I have a home among my own people.'

"What can be done for her?' Elisha asked. Gehazi said, 'Well, she has no son and her husband is old.'

Then Elisha said, 'Call her.' So he called her, and she stood in the doorway.

"About this time next year,' Elisha said, 'you will hold a son in your arms.'

"No, my lord,' she objected. 'Don't mislead your servant, O man of God!'

"But the woman became pregnant, and the next year about that same time she gave birth to a son, just as Elisha had told her.

"The child grew, and one day he went out to his father, who was with the reapers.

"'My head! My head!' he said to his father. His father told a servant, 'Carry him to his mother.'

"After the servant had lifted him up and carried him to his mother, the boy sat on her lap until noon, and then he died."

Did anyone in history have a greater reason to accuse God than this woman?

She never asked for the boy; it was Elisha's idea. She had learned to suppress her need to be a mother and had resigned herself to being childless. Her first response was, "Don't deceive me. Don't awaken in me a hope that ultimately will not be fulfilled."

Instead of being an occasion to attack God's character, she reversed the attack and threw it in Satan's face. She remembered that God doesn't awaken hope except to fulfill it. She resolved to fight back.

The meat of this message is the woman herself. What did she do during her sorrow of sorrows? How did she handle her grief? Most importantly, what was the outcome of her choices?

Crisis brings out the best or the worse in us. What it brought out in this woman is a treasure for the ages! It is a beacon for brokenhearted people for all time.

What did she do first? She immediately laid the dead child on the prophet's bed. This was her way of putting tragedy in God's hands.

She could have gripped the child in her arms and rocked back and forther hysterically wailing while she cursed God for the whole episode. The point is that she refused to be swallowed up asking, "Why? Why, God? How could you do this?"

I repeat: though it is very tempting to accuse God, don't do it!

Even though you desperately feel the need to know *why* this happened, it is more important, infinitely more important, to ask God what to do now! Asking "why" will plunge you into the quicksand of introspection. Asking "what" honors God and births a counterattack.

The following verses from I Samuel illustrate this point clearly:

"Now it happened when David and his men came to Ziklag, on the third day, that the Amalekites had invaded South and Ziklag, attacked Zilag and burned it with fire, and had taken captive the women and those who were there, from small to great they did not kill anyone, but carried them away and went their way. So David and his men came to the city, and there it was, burned with fire; and their wives, their sons, and their daughters had been taken captive.

Then David and the people who were with him lifted up their voices and wept, until they had no more power to weep. And David's two wives, Ahinoam the Jezreelitess, and Abigail the widow of Nabal the Carmelite, had been taken captive.

Now David was greatly distressed, for the people spoke of stoning him, because the soul of all the people was grieved, every man for his sons and daughters. But David strengthened himself in the Lord.

Then David said to Abiathar the priest, Ahimelech's son, 'Please bring the ephod here to me.' And Abiathar brought the ephod to David.

So David inquired of the Lord, saying, 'Shall I pursue this troop? Shall I overtake them?' And He answered him, 'Pursue, for you shall surely overtake them and without fail recover all.' (I Samuel 30:1-8)

David and his men found their homes burned down and their families missing. The men wept until they had no strength to weep.

Suddenly, David's life was ruined! His own men were about to murder him!

Verse 8 reveals David's vision of God's character; he encouraged himself in God. He did not ask "why?"; he asked for direction. "Shall I pursue them?" What bold words! God's reply was instant. He said, "Pursue, for you will surely overtake them and without fail recover all!"

David pursued the enemy. The Shunammite woman laid

the boy on the prophet's bed and then <u>pursued</u> the prophet.

My next point is summed up in three mighty words, "It is well."

When her husband asked the Shunammite woman why she was going to the prophet, she said, "*It is well.*" When Elisha saw her coming and sent Gehazi to ask if "all is well," she said, "It is well!"

The greatest threat to us in crisis is our own spirit. If we can control it, command it, and force it to say, "It is well," then Satan's major foothold is broken. We must learn to talk to our own emotions. We shouldn't ask God "why" but we need to ask our own spirit "why"!

> "Why are you cast down, O my soul? Any why are you disquieted within me?
>
> "Hope in God, for I shall yet praise Him." (Psalm 42:5b)

There it is! Command your spirit, then pursue the enemy!

The woman grabbed Elisha's feet in a death grip. She implored him to act.

The next point I want to make refers to contending. Modern Christians *have forgotten the art of contending.* We are discouraged far too easily! We give up fighting after the first resistance.

The battle for this boy's life had just begun. Elisha sent Gehazi bearing the prophet's staff; maybe death would respect the staff and the assistant! No way. Next, the prophet himself stretched over the dead child. Death loosened its grip but would not let go. Elisha paced back and forth, calling to the Lord. Suddenly he stretched over the child again, warring for his life. The child sneezed seven times. He was fully alive! Back from the stingy grave, back into his mother's arms! Hallelujah!

That miracle that was stolen was pulled back from the lion's mouth.

Let me rehearse the five things you do when Satan steals your miracle:

1. Immediately place the tragedy in God's hands.

2. Inquire of God, asking Him "What do I do? not "Why did you let this happen?"

3. Wait, expecting a clear direction; say to your spirit, "It is well."

4. Run with the plan as soon as it is revealed.

5. Contend for the victory. Demonstrate total resolve until the miracle is pulled back from Satan's mouth.

XVI. IF YOU DRINK ANYTHING DEADLY

"And delivered righteous Lot, who was oppressed by the filthy conduct of the wicked (for that righteous man, dwelling among them, tormented his righteous soul from day to day be seeing and hearing their lawless deeds)." (II Peter 2:7-8 NIV)

Dear Friends,

To be vexed means to be tormented continually either by lots of little things or by a sudden big crisis.

What is the value of an unvexed spirit? In this present darkness, it is life and death.

These final days have shifted the great threats to people from hunger, disease, and war; the great battlefield now is our emotions. We have created a monster; our culture cranks out unprecedented pressure and disappointment.

In Los Angeles, drivers at the boiling point shoot at each other. We see rage on the way to work, on the job, then again on the way home. Modern life is a case of every system being overloaded and every action being intensified as we race toward a high-tech nervous breakdown.

Some people have found way to cope that seem almost worse than the disease. Punkers sport clothes resembling nuclear war victims, turning up the music to nose-bleed levels. Others declare war on society by committing grisly murders that repulse even seasoned police officers. Still others spread AIDS deliberately, and the populace in general seems to be in a coma ignoring the threat, still reveling in casual sex. Network television responds with bolder sex scenes than ever before.

We are watching the emergence of the new barbarians. Vulgar, rude, loud, caustic and violent, they now permeate all parts of the society. Decent folk fight to move to good neighborhoods, only to find that the rabble is there too.

Ironically, the Christian can suffer more than the general populace. Modern life grates against everything we stand for. Jostling with this morally fallen society day after day is taxing our spirits. Without a solid anchor, we can become distorted and even broken. We can be twisted by the Sodom we live in. We can end up hating the lost we're supposed to reach or allow ourselves immorality because it seems tame compared to what the world revels in.

Christian parenting is now all-out war. A Christian teen now faces more temptation in a day than I remember facing in a year.

What can we do? How do we keep a sense of peace in this maelstrom?

The church is in desperate need of retrieving a truth that has served saints of God throughout the ages. This truth concerns our devotional life.

At one time the writings of men like Andrew Murray and A.W. Tozer seemed to be just for people who wanted to be deeper. They should be required reading for all Christians. Those whom we esteem to be spiritual giants were merely men and women pressed by crisis into discovering a way to draw abundant life from God in a secret place ... every day.

The first thing we must do is be convinced that such an experience does exist and is for us. We must believe in the oasis in the desert, where we find peace that the world cannot take away. We must be persuaded that God is a strong tower to run into and be washed of the toxic effect of modern life. The crushing element of today demands that if such a relationship is available, we seek it above all else.

The next step is not easy because it cuts to the heart of the meaning of the word "devotion." We must devote our waking hours to basking in His life-giving presence.

When I awake, the demands of my day want to drive me to feverish activity. I am a preacher; my job involves prayer, yet it is still a struggle to keep it a priority.

The laity struggles just as much. I appreciate this, but time for prayer must be found. Finding and claiming this daily treasure is half the battle. The other half is grasping this principle of daily renewal and cleansing.

When I worked in Berkeley, I constantly saw raw filth packaged as intellectual liberation. Repeated doses of this began to vex me deeply. Without relief, I would be squashed with despair.

God led me to a little book by David Wilkerson entitled I'M NOT MAD AT GOD. He related the same exact problem. His spirit writhed under the continual exposure to the degeneration on the streets of New York. He found a wonderful application for the promise in Mark 16:18: "If they drink any deadly thing it will by no means hurt them."

David Wilkerson argued that spiritual poison is as deadly a physical poison and this promise in Mark should apply. It did, and he found an artesian well of daily renewal. He felt an inner washing that restored peace and innocence.

It worked for him, it worked for me, and it will work for you. In years past this might have seemed like battlefield surgery exclusively for front-line saints, but today we all need it.

Possessing an unvexed spirit means subjugating the insane world we live in to the order of the kingdom of God.

Our prayer time must be transformed; it must no longer be just a time of loading the Lord with our list of needs. It must be a declaration of His majesty and dominion over the puny railings of men. What we are doing in prayer is the real living, anyway. Our chores, careers, appointments are secondary, almost symbolic ... prayer is literal! This is where wars are won, traps defused, and wisdom and direction imparted.

The issue is not the length of this devotion but the quality. You worship, you petition, you listen, and you emerge with power to triumph over the day.

Isaiah 50:4 says, "He awakens me morning by morning, He awakens my ear to hear as the learned."

A limitless reservoir awaits us: wisdom beyond Satan's craftiness, power beyond the world's insanity, and love above and beyond the scope of our daily trials.

XVII. FINAL VICTORY OVER FEAR

Dear Friends,

You may remember President Reagan proposing a astonishing defense system for North America. From space, lasers would track and destroy enemy missiles. The Russians had a strange reaction to "star wars." They ridiculed the idea as impossible and at the same time they adamantly opposed our building it. This begs the question: if they were so convinced the system was impossible, why were they so strongly against our building it?

Similarly, Satan belittles our claims of a mighty life in the Spirit as impossible. He scoffs at our claim to transform neighborhoods. Yet he strives at every point to oppose and frustrate attempts toward these goals. If our plans and wishes had no chance of being realized, they would not be opposed. The flak we are taking proves we are on to something significant. That is why there is a special attack on all of us at this moment.

The letters that I have received lately asking for prayer have revealed something significant. There is an attack on people to paralyze their faith. Sudden fear grips them and they feel suffocated with despair. Fear is the main dragon of modern life. It is a many-headed monster that challenges all of us. It affects us in ways we don't realize. It can make us withdraw from friends; it can rob us of our appetite or make us overeat. Dread and fear can make your whole body ache and leave you exhausted all the time. And you may not suspect that the real culprit is a deep-seated fear.

Believers have tried many of the latest trends in doctrine to relieve their agony but no relief has come. So prevalent is the wave of anxiety that I can safely say that you are either under attack now or will be soon. So with you in mind, I went to prayer and study about a true biblical response to fear. I wanted to write you something that would help, not just bless!

While mining for gold in the book of Ephesians, I found that the system of defense that the Pentagon wants for America already exists for all the children of God in the spirit. There is a star wars defense system already in place. This system is poised against the "flaming arrows of Satan."

Next I took the evidence of these fear warheads and saw that they fell into three categories. Before I tell you what they are and how to deal with them, you must do the first and foremost act of defense against fear. You must set up this system over your soul.

"Put on the whole armor of God" is a clear command and no believer can ignore it. Hear me! Being born again is no exemption from crisis. It is a life force within you that can respond to daily attacks. By the use of real faith, we ward off every fear.

The beginning of permanent victory is the living realization of what John said in his epistle, "Perfect love casts out all fear." The first piece of armor we put on is the persuasion that God loves unconditionally and that his love is concrete. It is always present and will, with our cooperation, avenge any thing satanic. The entire biblical system of defense is built upon this truth. The rest is a matter of enforcing the peace of Christ, which is to rule over your spirit.

So now let's face three warheads of fear and examine the Bible for proper reactions to them:

1. **Condemnation**

After Christians sin, they fear God's anger and withdraw from God. It is amazing how many people no longer pray or fellowship with other Christians because they have sinned. It is human nature to avoid someone we have failed but spiritually it is disastrous. Satan gets you alone and begins to gossip about God to you. In this state of isolation, he can wound you deeply.

Here is a wonderful truth! You have sinned, but do not turn away! Don't be afraid. God is pleased to make you His people!

When God saved you, he knew what He was getting. Our weaknesses may shock us but not Jesus. Get up! Get back in the race. The proper response to condemnation is to immediately run to God for forgiveness.

"If we confess our sins, He is faithful and just to forgive us our sins, and to cleanse us from all unrighteousness." (I John 1:9)

The only people who don't fall are those who stay down. The shocking discovery you will make if you go

98

back to prayer is how glad God is to see you.

2. **The Flood of Calamity**

Something outrageous beyond your control comes crashing down on your life. This is a time when several problems combine to destroy us suddenly. To add to the perplexity, this tidal wave may strike right after a time of victory in order to catch us completely off guard. The enemy's goal? Panic ... unbridled panic.

What is the Bible's antidote to this vicious tactic? In order to expose Satan and see the answer, let me take you back to that moment when Moses was backed up to the Red Sea. He had just liberated a nation out of slavery by miracles only now to be ambushed with no escape. As the Egyptian chariots were bearing down, panic seemed the only response, but God's order came as clear as a bell, "Stand still and see the salvation of God."

The answer is that if something attacks me and I have no response, it means that the next move is God's, not mine. I am to stand still. Jehoshaphat faced a similar disaster in Jerusalem. The children of Ammon, Moab and Mount Seir had allied to destroy all of Judah. The king said in prayer, "We have no might against the host but our eyes are on you." Once again the order came by prophecy from heaven, "You shall not need to fight in this battle. The battle is mine, said the Lord."

When fear makes you paralyzed, that is when you move. When fear makes you want to move in fear, that is when you stand still. Always react opposite to fear, not with it. So when something vile, unjust and overwhelming strikes suddenly, it means it is God's battle and a response must not come from you because a response is about to come from heaven

3. **Fear of Change or Adventure**

The two fear tactics we have already covered are fears that can be easily diagnosed since they are brought on by more obvious circumstances. This last one is subtle but just as dangerous because it can paralyze us by unconscious behavior.

The symptom of this fear is a withdrawal into a predictable routine. We don't want to venture out or risk. In the world, in its extreme manifestation, this is known as agoraphobia. People afflicted with agoraphobia are terrified to walk out of their home!

Christians are afraid to venture into new living, to change negative relationships, to risk finding a career that challenges their talents.

Superficial analysis might conclude that we fear failure so we retreat to safety. The real issue is much deeper.

The big reason relates directly to recent history. We have been repeatedly shattered by tragedy. Monuments of security have crumbled. We have come to believe that anything can happen, from a bank failure to the explosion of the space shuttle. However, we have overreacted and we have distorted the danger of change.

What has hurt the church s that some leaders have fed the fear rather than exposed it. By emphasizing personality needs to the exclusion of teaching final victory over fear, ministers can reinforce feelings of inadequacy. Many believers today do not witness, do not pursue excellence because they believe they are in a prolonged program of healing of their emotions.

The cry of the church must not simply be, "Be patient, God is not finished with me yet," but also the biblical cry, "Through our God we shall do valiantly!"

What must be realized is that the principal cause of this fear is the lack of knowing that God is with us. We must take risks to see greatness. We must venture into the unknown to make a difference. We must pierce regions of Satan to see triumph! That means an occasional detour through the valley of the shadow of death.

Yea, though I walk through the valley of the shadow of death, I will fear no evil for You are with me. Your rod and Your staff, they comfort me." (Psalm 23:4)

We must have a granite confidence in God's commitment to us! He will always be with us.

Joshua was commissioned to go forward but his strength was knowing God was with him. "No man shall be able to stand before you all the days of your life; as I was with Moses, so I will be with you. I will not leave your nor forsake you." (Joshua 1:5)

Now hear this important conclusion. Why is fear such

a repeated tool of Satan? Because he is a dethroned despot. He must use our own imaginations to scare us. Jesus broke him! His threats are phantoms and specters meant to intimidate you to inferior, harmless discipleship.

Three times in the wilderness Jesus answered Satan with scripture. Let us take His example; let us study our response to Lucifer; let us raise the sword of the Spirit and watch fear disintegrate!

Shall we have children, build homes, perfect our talents! Or shall we tiptoe silently, reluctantly, like frightened children, into the future?

When Jesus said to occupy until He comes, He meant we are to live enthusiastically. With problems, yes! With attacks, yes! But no fear or dread should break our pace or lessen our zest for adventure. For us, each day shines brighter to a more perfect day. For Satan, it is one more day on death row as the executioner draws nearer.

The defense system against fear is set over us now. It's up to us to start practicing the promises that make it work!

XVIII. THE KEYS TO YOUR HEALING MIRACLE

Dear Friends,

Sickness, life-threatening sickness, can evoke feelings of rage, grief, helplessness, and confusion all at once. Worse still, seeking healing in the church today can be its own emotional trauma. We are bombarded with advice; some of it is discouraging and some of it is simply dangerous.

It is truly embarrassing and shameful to watch hurting people caught in the crossfire of "teachings" and insensitive remarks.

For twenty-five years I have watched miracles in our crusades. While others around me rejoiced, I had mixed emotions. My heart grieved for those who weren't healed. Night after night, people would come and leave as sick as when they came. To be sure, many were healed and God's power was undeniable. Still I would retire to my room to weep and ask, "Why?" My search lasted years.

This letter embodies the answer I finally received. Some of the truths I am going to share came by thunderous revelation where the heavens seemed to open and God's glory drenched me. Other nuggets were found by mining patiently from the great vessels of God and permitting the Holy Spirit to wash away the corruptions of the flesh.

Have I solved all mysteries about healing? Of course not. Many questions remain and will until heaven; but this I do know: I am prepared and determined to give you the best of what I have learned, and moreover, I want to take you the the Master Himself with great confidence in His mercy and power.

Walk with me now as we journey to a miracle.

• KEY #1: Remove the unreasonables.

To enter God's presence means you first take out the trash — the unreasonables, as I call them Let me explain. I do not, for example, believe in God simply because I know He's there, but because Atheism is unreasonable. The universe is too orderly to be an accident. It is equally unreasonable to declare war on the Bible. A tradition can scream all it wants that God doesn't want to heal us, but that is unreasonable since the scriptures are replete with declarations of His total desire to give health. *He wants to heal, period.*

Miracles verses are too numerous to cite here, so let me showcase just Psalms 103:2,3: "Bless the Lord, O my soul, And forget not all His benefits: Who forgives all your iniquities, Who heals all your diseases..."

Remove the opposite "unreasonable" that presumes God must heal us at our beck and call. This extreme has caused people to forego medication and other dangerous acts trying to force God to act. We are not to tempt God!

Other unreasonables include belief in unseen family curses that hinder healing, that our faith is weak, or any petty technicality. God is great and faithful to reveal our hindrances

104

"...an if anything you think otherwise, God will reveal even this to you". (Philippians 3:15)

Simply put, we must face the fact that we need a miracle and enter His presence without any baggage. At first letting go of healing superstition is scary, but it can bring great relief.

Admitting we don't know why, yet honoring Jesus as the rewarder of those who diligently seek Him, has untold power to avail! **Come to Him with neither presumption nor insecurity.**

Mark 6 is very important on this subject. Because they did not honor Jesus, it says in verse 5: "Now He could do no mighty work there, except that He laid His hands on a few sick people and healed them."

Note that it says He *could not*, it does not say *would not*. This means He wanted to heal but their *unreasonable* attitude blocked Him.

Have you ever noticed that when you have good friends over for dinner that no matter how long you are together talking, the really meaningful conversation doesn't start until you are all standing at the front door ready to say good-night?

Jesus said, "Behold I stand at the door and knock..." He knocks at the door of our misconceptions. Open the door! It is time for a heart-to-heart talk with Jesus where nothing comes between you and Him. He knocks on the door of our preconceptions. Open up! It's time for a heart-to-heart talk with your Healer.

• KEY #2: Ask Correctly.

"Now they came to Jericho. As He went out of Jericho with His disciples and a great multitude, blind Bartimaeus, the son of Timaeus, sat by the road begging. And when he heard that it was Jesus of Nazareth, he began to cry out and say, "Jesus, Son of Daivd, have mercy on me!" (Mark 10:46-47)

Bartimaeus remains for all time the purest example of anyone who has ever asked for healing from Jesus.

First, notice that he cried for mercy. **Healing is first and last an act of mercy.** Some will retort that healing is guaranteed in the atonement so we do not need to plead for mercy. **Healing is in the atonement just as salvation is — a provision we did not earn or deserve.**

Anyone who approaches God claiming *rights* rejection. This attitude offends and breaks the heart of God because it shows, at best, ignorance, and at worst, ingratitude for what happened on the cross. When we were helpless, Christ died for us. This was unspeakable love that even stunned the angels.

When it comes to healing, we are again helpless. Some dare to spout healing verses at God meaning to enforce the contract. They do this out of fear and doubt and call it faith.

They grab hold of a principle because they fear trusting God as a person. The cross not only shows us how to ask, it reveal*Who* we are asking.

Romans 8:32 says: "He who did not spare His own Son,

106

but delivered Him up for us all, how shall He not with Him also freely give us all things?"

Please focus on the words, "He who did not spare His own son." Paul wants us to see this amazing person behind the promises. This gaze of the soul gives us a long-awaited, unfiltered view of the glory of Jesus and of God the Father, until in confidence, true supernatural confidence, we cry out.

Look at the next phrase: "How shall He not with Him also freely give us all things?"' The cross is proof positive — God will **not withhold.** After all He has done, how shall He not! Say it, "How shall He not!" Again, "How shall He not along with Him also freely give us all things."

Bartimaeus could not stop crying out once He saw the full measure of this willing, loving, and consuming fire which was Jesus. He lost all fear. He left his garment; he knew that his heart's desire would not be denied. But He has one last lesson on asking.

Jesus says to Bartimaeus, "What do you want me to do for you?" Isn't it obvious what a blind man needs? **We must specify! We must verbalize...a miracle must be welcomed...we must ask.** The crowd is hushed as Bartimaeus cried once more, "That I might receive my sight." The Word says, "Immediately he received his sight!"

- **KEY #3: Jesus gives you the faith to be healed.**

What is the gift called faith? What is this mysterious force so mighty that just a trace element of it can cast a mountain into the sea?

We will not completely understand it in this life, and to believe we will is the height of self-delusion.

The only certainty we have is what Hebrews says: "Looking unto Jesus the author and finisher of our faith."

In essence, faith is a deposit of God Himself that removes all human interference to a miracle. Human belief is endless work; faith is an effortless confidence. **When this God-quality appears, a miracle will follow.** Wherever faith is present, Jesus will honor it.

In Matthew 15, a woman begs Jesus to heal her demon-possessed daughter. **He denies her request:** "It is not right to take the children's bread and give it to the dogs."

By this, Jesus illustrated the destiny of the Jews as the heirs of the household and how that, after the cross, the rest of the world would be blessed.

But the woman's reply is the key: "True Lord, but even the dogs eat the crumbs that fall off of the master's table." (Matthew 15:27)

There it is for you and me! While His teaching was directed at Jews, "bread" had fallen off the table to this Gentile woman's soul. Jesus tells us what that bread is — "Oh, woman, great is your **faith!**" Her daughter was delivered in that instant.

We can use our own "faith" and be frustrated, or we can take the bread from Jesus and make it our own.

Can you see why I am so adamant about keeping Jesus at

the center of our quest for a miracle?

Cease from all your own labor. Let the Holy Spirit usher you to Jesus. There, in quiet trust, wait and expect faith to be imparted. He will not deny you!

• KEY #4: The Flashpoint of Your Miracle.

One truth is left to embrace. At the moment that faith comes, something happens: **You must act! All faith ends in an act.**

The voice of the Lord will become clear; but what He commands you to do may startle you. The actions God requires to release miracles are mysteriously unique to each person.

- **Jesus ordered one man to wash mud off of his eyes.**
- **The ten lepers had to go show themselves to the priests.**
- **Hezekiah was told to put a poultice on his boil.**

The list is endless, but each has a purpose. Somehow, in a way that only God understands, these flashpoints set us free! This is something that we may not know about ourselves.

Naaman, the leper, seemed so willing to do anything to be healed yet he became enraged at the Prophet's words that simply ordered him to dip seven times in the Jordan River.

"But Naaman became furious, and went away and said, 'Indeed, I said to myself, "He will surely come out to me, and stand and call on the name of the Lord his God, and wave his hand over the place, and heal the leprosy."

Are not the Abanah and the Pharpar, the rivers of Damascus, better than all the waters of Israel? Could I not wash in them and be clean?" So he turned and went away in a rage". (II Kings 5:11-12)

Naaman was healed of far more than leprosy. This flashpoint revealed the root of his problem!

Did this command truly perturb Naaman because it touched the root of his nationalism, pride, and his contempt for Israel? His servant implored him, "...had the prophet asked you to do something great, would you not have done it? How much more than, when he says to you, 'Wash, and be clean?'"

The act that follows your gift of faith may very well grate your flesh, but in the doing of it comes *a miracle.*

In conclusion, it's just Jesus and you now, and what a powerful place that is to be!

Your flashpoint will be different. Bear the offense! Obey the Holy Spirit! Never forget, this is the most trustworthy Person in the universe.

There they are, my friends, keys to your healing miracle. Jesus stands before you now, tender yet awesome. Surrender to Him. Cast out theories, theologies, formulas, and methods. Let Him be all in all! **He will bring your miracle.**